"Outstanding, moving, touching … You will cry, you will be surprised, you will be taught, and finally guided. Excellent book for people with cancer, serious medical problems and just people who are lost in everyday busy, crazy life. "Message from the Black Swan" is a sweet raisin in the salty ocean of real life."

Natalia Lazik, M.D., Ph.D.

"*Message from the Black Swan* is FANTASTIC! I wish that this book were in the hands of everybody with a cancer diagnosis! For those who are truly searching, looking beneath the surface, not accepting the medical protocol as the only way, this book offers profound guidance. It is a pleasure to read, it flows like a river, and the author makes sense of an astonishingly vast amount of material. The credibility of being a medical doctor undergoing this transformation is impeccable! Marina's journey conveys the clearest demonstration I have ever seen that we are mind-body-spirit, and healing must address all three aspects."

Laurel Eisenschiml, RN.

"Dr. Wassermann is making a great contribution based on her own experience to people who suffer of cancer with the "Body-Mind-Spirit interconnection and involvement model". Not only the body needs to be healthy, not only in cancer, but in any illnesses, and her approach of this model is amazingly clear and certain."

Alejandro Jorrin, M.D.

"This book brings a profound paradigm shift in our thinking and the way we have seen the world of cancer treatment. This book is a revelation: it gives us knowledge and resources to use as a reference in order to make the best choice to heal cancer from within. The book is a remarkable and important contribution towards healing cancer modalities. The practical approach shown in the book leads us to acknowledge that the "ancient genius" is always inside each one of us; it transforms the comprehensive healing of mind, body and spirit into a magical guide for all those diagnosed with any incurable disease."

Irina Urben, M.D.

"I found this book to be a moving and astonishing account of Marina's search for healing. The concept of the whole self and the physical and spiritual being crucially interrelated was fascinating, and it seemed to me that this would be an excellent read for anyone who feels they need to find peace within themselves, either to heal themselves physically or mentally. Marina's own inner strength and optimism was something that shone through. The way she saw cancer as an opportunity, a quest to improve herself is probably the most startling and profound aspect of the book."

Daniela Morini

"The book is very powerful. The story is really incredible! Most striking and impressive is Marina's positive attitude in the situation where it is almost impossible to be positive, her strong belief that she WILL survive and get well, and her hard work toward the goal!"

Yelena Mel, M.D.

Message from the Black Swan

A Medical Doctor's Journey
To Healing Truth Through Cancer

Marina Wassermann, M.D.

This book is dedicated to all who've been beside me during this challenging time, offering their help, with my deep gratitude.

The author of this book does not dispense medical advice or prescribe the use of any technique as a form of treatment for physical, emotional, or medical problems without the advice of a physician. It is not intended to replace your relationship with your health care providers nor should you stop taking any medications. Always seek the advice of a physician regarding any mental, physical or emotional condition. In the event you use any of the information in this book for yourself, the author and the publisher assume no responsibility for your actions.

TABLE OF CONTENTS

INTRODUCTION

"There are two mistakes one can make along the road to truth ... not going all the way, and not starting." —Buddha

Dear Reader:

I'm about to share with you the experiences and discoveries I've made during my cancer journey. I sincerely believe that tens of thousands of people—not only those who are facing incurable diseases, but everyone who has any health issues or feels stuck in their routine life with ongoing problems—can benefit tremendously from this book.

Being a medical doctor, and always having believed in the power of traditional medicine, I had to go through this rigorous trial to find an *inner* power, one that every human being has, in order to heal.

During my journey I realized that when you have cancer, you are the only one who remains one-on-one with the incurable disease. It is *you* who are responsible for the choices you're making. Trying to find the "way out" and searching for answers to my questions, I found tons of information related to cancer healing, but I felt that for an ordinary person going through this life crisis, it would be far too easy to get lost in a sea of information.

I wanted to understand the *core principles of healing*.

While searching for answers, I was vigorously involved in all possible modalities of cancer healing at the body-mind-spirit level, going through a tremendous experience that led me to deep inner transformation—and, as a result, caused changes in my world perception. Through this profound insight I learned to find the truth, as well as the answers to all my questions.

In this book, I'll be offering you clear guidance on fundamental principles of the body-mind-spirit ideology—a road map for your journey that will lead you to your own healing. If life is challenging you in any way, this guidance will serve as your navigator.

The systemic approach of body-mind-spirit introduced in the book will give you the whole picture of this unity, its meaning, importance, interconnection, and influence on your life. You will be able to discover the key principles for your healing—and with this knowledge, you'll be able to make *your* choice, from your own comfort zone.

For more than a thousand years, false beliefs about our identity, about who it is that we truly are, have kept us in a prison of illusion: it never allowed us to win over cancer. But the truth is that *you* can awake your inner power and heal yourself from cancer, and this book will guide you toward it.

I hope that I'm going to touch your hearts and trigger some healing power in you as well.

PART I:

Stepping Into the Journey

CHAPTER ONE:

Facing Cancer

"Faith is believing what you don't see; the reward of this faith is to see what you believe."
—Saint Augustine

I would never have thought—after going through all the challenges of immigration, studies, and hard work to pursue the career of medical doctor in the U.S., once I was very close to my dream—that I would end up with cancer.

My practice in life has always been to face challenges with acceptance and gratitude. I've always thanked God for the opportunity to learn and grow, for the opportunity to become stronger and wiser. But this time it was so hard to acknowledge anything positive about this situation.

I remember the day I got the news; I knelt down immediately and prayed. In my prayers, I accepted this trial with gratitude—as I'd always done with everything that happened to me before—and I thanked God

3

for my path, promising to learn what I needed to in order to go through whatever turns it might take.

Oddly enough, I didn't have any fear of death at all; somewhere deep in my soul I knew that I was healthy and that I needed to embark upon a journey to find the answer to the question that was in my heart: *What is love?*

It wasn't the first time I'd asked that question. It was in fact a question I'd asked over and over again throughout all my life: what is the art of love, and how can I reach it? How I can get in touch with the harmony of the universe, and give it to others? What does pure *love*—among parents, children, family members, friends, colleagues and myself—feel and look like? If it isn't an emotion, sex, or ego approval, but trust, understanding, giving-ness, with no thoughts of receiving anything in return, loving the other one the way they are ... then how I can get there?

I was looking for the answer to this question all my life, trying very hard to "mother" the world through support and understanding while swallowing and suppressing my own painful emotions. I was ignoring and humiliating my soul's needs, to the point that one day I became numb—and not only to myself, but also to others.

I'd always been an optimistic person who inspired others, and yet I reached the point when I became indifferent to the surrounding world, dying inside and not even really understanding why ...

And then it happened.

On March 21, 2011, when I was doing my third year of medical residency in the United States, I was diagnosed with stage-three breast cancer, 9.3 centimeters by 3.5 centimeters in size, with metastases under my arm.

I was shocked, to say the least. At 47 years old, I'd always been a balanced, positive and resilient person, with a physically active, healthy lifestyle; I'd never taken any medication, or smoked, or drunk alcohol. There were no other health-related issues. I regularly had annual routine checkups, including mammograms, which had always been normal.

And then I found a lump in my breast, and went to see a doctor. This part is difficult to believe, but even then the 10-centimeter lump didn't show up on the mammogram! These tests indicated that everything was normal. Only a follow-up ultrasound with a biopsy confirmed that it was cancer; the breast MRI indicated the real size of the tumor.

All my tests, including biopsies, CT scans, MRIs, US, bone scans, and blood tests were done within two days. Professionals from my work hospital saw me at once; they told me I would need a year of chemotherapy, along with surgery and radiation. I was also told that I couldn't wait more than two weeks, since cancer cells spread easily. I was therefore immediately scheduled for a bilateral mastectomy with follow-up chemotherapy at my work place.

I was in shock. I was functioning entirely on autopilot.

One thing I should note that happened immediately was the tremendous support I received from my residency program, my program director, my colleagues, and my friends. I was touched by people's compassion and willingness to help.

There was an ICU nurse in particular with whom I'd felt a connection in the past. We always talked about doing something together but just hadn't found the time. I remember one day I was walking with my husband and we happened to see her; but neither of us was alone, so I didn't say anything then about what had been happening; I just said hello and we passed by.

But she stopped and called me back. "Has something happened?"

I didn't say anything. I couldn't trust my voice.

"Can I hug you?" she asked, seeing that I couldn't speak. I just nodded. She gathered me in her arms and I could feel it, her love and her caring. I buried my head into her shoulder and whispered my diagnosis.

Immediately she, too, was crying. She took my face in her hands. "No, it isn't true! Not you … not you!" I could sense her pain, her love, her compassion. She was offering me her help and I assured her that soon I would be back.

It seemed that God was putting specific people into my life for guidance.

I needed to reflect and recharge before I took any major steps. During those days my close friend from Canada, Annie, was tracing my every step, calling me several times every day and trying to guide me through the mental fog I was experiencing.

I had only two weeks left and I was trying to find my way out of this misery. Somewhere deep in my heart I still hoped for a miracle to happen. I'd been seen by a plastic surgeon; I'd talked to my colleagues who were competent in this area, looking through research on all available treatments. I met with two women who'd had breast cancer and kindly agreed to show me what their breasts looked like after plastic surgery. Finally I decided to go for a second opinion and ended up making an appointment at Massachusetts General Hospital in Boston.

And I still hadn't found the right path for navigating my journey.

Annie was supplementing my own research with as much of the latest scientific data as possible. I had to be able to make the right choices— but I had limited time and a myriad of things to consider.

And I was scared.

My fear wasn't about pain or even death, believe it or not. What I was afraid of was making decisions in a very short period of time and what the effect of those decisions would be on my loved ones, on our quality of life in the long run. It was important for me to feel peace during— and after—my surgeries.

And it wasn't just me; my husband and son had been catapulted along with me into this situation with all its uncertainties and they both needed support too. They remained silent and were doing whatever was needed on autopilot too. It seemed that the news had been an even greater shock to them than it was to me.

Before my trip to Boston, my husband and I went home to Canada for a few days.

Annie had printed out a lot of information we needed to read through together, and in addition she'd made some appointments for me—one with a priest and another with a well-known Chinese doctor who'd successfully treated cancer patients with herbs.

The appointment with the Chinese doctor was unsettling. He offered to cure my cancer within six to eight weeks with herbs and applications—if only I would not "cut off," as he phrased it, my breast.

He showed me proof of his claim: a journal with pictures of women from all over the world (accompanied by official tests, data and results) whom he'd cured from different stages of breast cancer, including women in "terminal" stages on whom regular western medicine had been unsuccessful.

I say the visit was unsettling, because now I had a dilemma: should I postpone surgery and try this eastern method? But I'd been a medical doctor for more than 20 years, and I didn't truly believe in the power of alternative medicine, despite his apparent evidence of healing. I didn't want to take that kind of risk, and decided to stick to the standard medical protocol of chemotherapy, surgery and radiation.

In order to be ready to go through the "transition period" easily, Annie arranged for us to go buy a wig made from human hair— of a color and style close to my own—and I began to wear it. She also printed out a lot of research materials on the latest scientific achievements in the field of plastic surgery and radiation, along with a practical manual for women with breast cancer. Annie also gave me some Flavin 7 Gold with Immune 7X mushrooms, which had been shown through research to be very effective in boosting the immune-system during chemotherapy.

I felt equipped to take the next step on my journey.

We left Canada and arrived in Boston for our meeting with the Massachusetts General Hospital (MGH) breast-cancer specialists who were using a multidisciplinary approach to patient care. I had only two days left before my surgery and didn't know what to expect.

At MGH, I met with a team of amazing women: an oncologist, a surgeon, and a radiologist. They spent a few hours with me discussing different therapy approaches. At this time of confusion and despair I was impressed by their professionalism, true compassion and open discussion on the various possibilities of treatment in my particular case.

Like most people, I've always felt that breasts are a symbol of womanhood, of beauty, and maybe even of security, and "cutting" it off felt that I was somehow losing all that. Now I was being given a chance to start with chemotherapy, not surgery, and the words of hope resonated deeply in me, bringing me back from the brink to a feeling of safety again. Those words became my anchors, my lifelines, and I held on to them for dear life.

At least I had another five months before surgery and radiation.

CHAPTER TWO:

Seeking the Way Out

"You will find peace not by trying to escape your problems, but by confronting them courageously. You will find peace not in denial, but in victory."
—J. Donald Walters

I started chemotherapy on April 4, 2011.

The plan for the first two months was for me to be on one regimen of chemotherapy, followed by a different one for the following three months, with subsequent surgery, radiation, and seven more months of chemo.

My residency program was very supportive, and I was given a chance to go through the first regimen of chemo treatment while staying at home. It would have been impossible for me to stay in the hospital around sick patients and anyway, I was experiencing all the possible side effects and my immune system was compromised. The idea was for me to return in June to resume my duties.

During the first week of chemo there was some nausea, weakness, and chills. My mediport (a central venous line implanted under the skin for long-term use during chemotherapy) became infected and a thrombus developed in my right internal jugular vein, so they added blood thinners.

I was looking for a way out, searching for the answer through doing internet research, and ordering books written by cancer survivors and medical experts on how I could get well on this journey.

Annie was doing the same, and pretty soon we had the latest scientific data for cancer treatment. We found the leading world centers and clinics in North America, Europe, and Asia that used advanced scientific approaches in the treatment of cancer patients. The differences between them were really only in deviation from the standard protocol by using additional modalities within the body-mind-spirit approach—things like detoxification, herbs, infrared sauna, diet, yoga, meditation, ect. The United States was the most conservative toward herb treatment with the least deviation, then Europe and Asia, and they all showed some success; but nobody could guarantee a cure.

I continued chemotherapy, along with doing what felt like endless research. I was expecting my sister Irina to come from Michigan and stay with me for two weeks until my husband could be with me. He and I had emigrated from Kazakhstan in 2003; now my husband and son were staying at our home in Canada while I did my residency in the United States. They were supposed to be on-duty, so to speak, until my parents arrived from Kazakhstan. Irina, my mother, and I had all been medical doctors back in Kazakhstan. Irina had pursued a career as a dermato-venereologist; my mother and I were neurologists and both practiced acupuncture.

During the past few years, Irina had been living in Michigan, following her own spiritual path, and her arrival triggered a shift in my consciousness.

We'd always been close to each other, but for the last two years our relationship hadn't been going well. Now my disease had brought us together again, and somehow all the misunderstandings were washed away, our souls were purified of all the offenses that had been committed, and we were learning to forgive. I was happy to see her again and felt comfortable around her. She brought me a lot of materials related to the body-mind-spirit approach and began to introduce me to that way of thinking.

What I realized during that time was that there was a great deal of information on the body-mind-spirit approach available through the internet, books, trainings, video, CDs, and so on. Everyone seemed to be very aware of it, and yet I still couldn't get a deep understanding of how it worked. I felt it was easy for an ordinary person to become lost in that sea of information. There wasn't any clear guidance to point toward fundamental principles of body-mind-spirit ideology and to introduce it as a system, showing meaning, importance, and interconnection, along with correlation and influence on a human life. And it certainly wasn't clear how and why some people could heal from cancer, but others didn't.

In spite of the fact that I'd decided to go with a standard protocol and was receiving chemotherapy, I still wasn't ready either for surgery or radiation, and was trying to find a way out. The chemotherapy side effect now was taking over me and I began to lose my hair.

I looked a little like a slightly shabby cat.

Irina was cutting my hair shorter and shorter, until one day she just shaved it off. Since I'd been wearing my wig from the first day, nobody realized that it wasn't my natural hair. It certainly puzzled the medical staff members taking care of me, until I finally told them the truth!

I felt tremendous respect for my oncologist, and trusted him implicitly: I kept telling him my cancer was going to go away, and that he would be able to present my case as an interesting one at the upcoming hospital conferences. He smiled.

Somewhere deep in my soul I still strongly held the conviction that I was healthy, and that the reason I had cancer was to find the answer to what love is—although I didn't understand why I had to be sick with an incurable disease in order to get there.

I felt that from the viewpoint of a logical mind all these statements were weird, but it was a truth for my soul. I was so convinced that I felt like shouting out, "this is so obvious, why don't you believe it?"

I was convinced; but so many questions remained. *Where do I need to start? In which direction do I need to go? To whom would I tell this? What would people think about me, a woman who'd been a doctor for many years and was now looking for love and talking nonsense?*

So I decided to share my feelings only with family members and close friends. My husband, to whom I'd been married for 25 years, was someone who'd always shown sober judgment and saw the world through the eyes of a logical mind. He just couldn't comprehend my search for love; and I understood him. Annie was supporting me, but did either of us really understand what we were doing and what it meant? And then there was Irina: throughout my chemotherapy, I kept telling her confidently that I was healthy; I remember that she looked at me and asked, "Are you aware how serious your disease is?"

I was more than aware, of course; but still nobody could either shake my belief—or reassure me. Irina advised me to at least start reading books about love, to pray, and search for answers.

I followed her advice and ordered books describing the concept of love; they included Erich Fromm's *The Art of Loving*, *The Heart's Code* by Paul Pearsall, and many others. I also began to do daily guided meditations, and I resumed yoga so I could create inner well-being. My colleagues from the hospital and residency program were visiting me, providing me with emotional and financial support, and I was impatient to go back to work.

Time flew by very quickly. Irina and I read books, listened to CDs, and spent a lot of time talking together. It was a valuable time for me to look at cancer, not from the logical perspective of a medical doctor's mind, but through the prism of my heart and soul.

What we discovered was that in order to heal from cancer, people had to make drastic changes in their lives, including, if necessary, changing one's physical location, and/or job, and/or relationships. Survivors went through a transformation process to find a new identity; sometimes they even changed how they looked physically.

During one such discussion, I told Irina that I would fight the cancer—but that I was not going to lose my family, and I would finish my residency anyway.

If I'd only known then how this journey was going to unfold for me.

Irina suggested that I shouldn't fight the cancer, but rather learn to love it. This was a new and very important concept, though it wasn't until later that I got a full understanding of its significance in the healing process.

Later on Irina advised me to begin to keep a diary. "You'll need it for your future book!" she said. I didn't take this very seriously, although I couldn't ignore the fact of her intuition and her ability to connect with the Source, since I was a witness and participant of one unbelievable story that happened to our family.

Many years before, our father, who had always been perfectly healthy, one day became acutely ill and started bleeding profusely. Nobody knew the cause of his condition. He was bleeding from his mouth, nose, and rectum; he urinated blood and developed widespread hemorrhages. By the third day, his condition had become critical, despite intensive treatment and transfusions; he could hardly breathe. His tongue looked like a bloody gag in his mouth and we were trying to feed him through a straw with a syringe.

Three of us (our mother, Irina, and I) were next to him all the time, doing the best we could to save his life. His diagnosis was not clear. It looked like DIC (Disseminated Intravascular Coagulopathy – pathologic activation of the blood coagulation system leading to blood clots in various organs, causing multiple organ failure and bleeding), but none of the blood tests confirmed any known disease and nobody was sure what it was.

The medical doctors and hematologists only shrugged; they said they'd never seen anything like it before. As his breathing was getting more labored, we knew we couldn't do much, and a feeling of helplessness set in. He couldn't be intubated (due to edema, bleeding, and airway blockage by the tongue) so we were given limited options: either let him die, or try to prolong his life with a tracheotomy (a surgical procedure which creates an airway through the neck into the windpipe) which didn't feel right to us.

That night, when he began gasping for air—with his open mouth blocked by his edematous red tongue—unable to say anything, but speaking to us only with his eyes, holding our hands in his own bruised hands, mother and I rushed him in desperation to the hospital's surgical department for a tracheotomy; but Irina stayed in the ward. We continued to watch him closely, still feeling that in his situation surgery wasn't the right choice. Within the next hour, his breathing became better and we brought him back to the ward.

When we arrived, Irina was lying on the bed with a severe headache, looking ill. "You won't believe this," she said to me, "but all this time I've been praying, and I felt some connection with a Source during this meditative state. I was here, praying to God and asking Him to save father's life. I told God to take my life instead."

It was too much for me on that day. I gave her medication and let her sleep. Despite being exhausted, she couldn't sleep during the night, suffering from a terrible headache and asking me all the time to give her more medication; but it didn't work. In the morning, she looked very sick and developed uterine bleeding—while at the same time our father's condition improved tremendously. His breathing was much better, there was light in his eyes again, and he began to recover very rapidly. It seemed that during the night there had been a turning-point for him: his bleeding had stopped and all organ functions improved within the next two days. Nothing like that ever happened to him again and all future medical tests would return normal results.

Irina, on the other hand, was sick for the next eight weeks.

She went to medical doctors and took medication, but they couldn't stop the bleeding. Her condition was getting worse: she began to lose weight, became pale and so weak that she couldn't go to work and was finally hospitalized. The cause of the bleeding wasn't clear, nothing seemed to help her, and we didn't know what to do.

This continued until she decided to see an old woman who began to treat her with herbs and prayers … and her bleeding stopped.

Now, remembering this story, I asked her if she could go "there" and pray for me and ask for help. She looked at me quizzically. "I don't want to get your disease, Marina," she said. "But I'll ask for directions."

She closed herself in the room for prayers and meditation, and I was very curious what she would tell me the next day.

"I have a message for you," she told me the next morning. "You need to consult Dr. Schulze."

Neither of us had ever heard the name before.

CHAPTER THREE:

An Anchor to Cure

"If there is no struggle, there is no progress."
—Frederick Douglass

I found Dr. Schulze's personal story interesting.

He'd been diagnosed with a genetic heart deformity and heart disease when he was sixteen, but he declined open-heart surgery, found the inner strength and wisdom necessary to follow his soul ... and healed himself. He devoted his life to natural healing programs, saving the lives of thousands of people with incurable diseases in his own clinic in California. Now he was in Europe and didn't do any more consulting, but had made all his programs and products available on a website.[1]

I began to look through all his materials, to read his books, listen to his CDs, and watch his videos. While I was processing this information,

---

[1] (https://www.herbdoc.com/index.php/?c=1).

I felt excitement—and some relief—from the stories of so many people with incurable and chronic diseases who had healed themselves on his program.

From that first moment I trusted him, and knew that he was the one - out of all the other natural doctors - I wanted to follow.

Now there was another dilemma for me. I'd already been on chemotherapy for two weeks of a miserable rollercoaster of thoughts and emotions, and I knew that Dr. Schulze's vision of healing wasn't aligned with a combination of completely opposite approaches in cancer treatment. And it made sense. On one hand, you immerse yourself in herbal formulas and detoxification routines by cleansing, fasting, flushing your body, and boosting your immune system. On the other hand, you're doing the complete opposite with chemotherapy by overloading your body with very toxic drugs and killing your immune system.

I wasn't ready, either emotionally or psychologically, to stop chemotherapy and start his program on my own. I felt that to do this I needed his presence, support, and direction. I wrote him a letter, but he didn't respond.

During those days I was starting to experience new feelings. My mind and heart were arguing with each other. My mind was telling me: "Are you crazy? You have access to the 'best of the best' medicine in the world, based on advanced scientific achievements, free, and available for you with great support around you! Don't be foolish!"

My heart protested, "But where will you end up with this advanced treatment? Do you want to go through this misery of being poisoned, cut, and burned, just because others tell you that it's the best standard protocol and is scientifically approved? What about non-standard protocols with which people have being healed from cancer by using powerful natural programs? What about miracles? How do they happen? Can you give me an answer to this? If you are not afraid of death, then there is nothing for you to lose! Follow me, find your answer and you will be safe."

I had to make a choice.

I thought about the results of the research that Annie and I had done. We'd learned that there were a lot of places in the world, mostly in

Europe, where a combination of chemotherapy along with diet, herbs, and detoxification were being used, with promising results.

So I decided to follow my heart, and I ordered Dr. Schulze's package for incurable disease. It was my own decision and I felt that there was no need to share or discuss it with anyone. Nobody could give me the right advice or answers in this matter, and I was the only one fully responsible for it.

I'd already received chemotherapy twice, and it was time for Irina to leave, since my husband was coming back from Canada to take care of me. He wasn't yet aware of Dr. Schulze's program—nor of my intention to engage with it.

When he arrived, I was so excited to tell him about discovering Dr. Schulze; but he was skeptical about it. Since Dr. Schulze's program was very intensive and required the help and involvement of other people, I needed him to be on board, and the more I told him about it, the more curious—and open to it—he became. By the time I got my package, he was ready to help and be a participant in the program; at least he wasn't against it and kept a neutral attitude.

The program was built on the body-mind-spirit approach and included a strict diet (only fresh juice with herbal tea for the first two weeks or even more—the longer, the better—after which the person can gradually start on a vegan diet), cleansing and detoxification of major organs (bowel, liver, kidney), bloodstream, body tissue and the lymphatic system from accumulated poisons, cancer cells, and toxic chemicals. It also included hydrotherapy three times a day, skin brushing, affirmations, visualizations, deep breathing, exercise and cold-sheet treatment.

The program was scheduled so that you start your day at 7am and have a task to do every fifteen to thirty minutes until 10pm. My days all started at six am and ended at 11 pm, since in addition to this program I put in meditations, yoga, and reading. Usually in the morning I drove to a lake surrounded by a big park area close to my home, doing yoga, breathing, saying positive affirmations while walking and enjoying nature.

We both stayed busy. I continued the program and in spite of being on very strong chemotherapy, I felt reasonably well. The hardest part of the program was the cold-sheet treatment, which was used by ancient people and recognized as one of the most powerful healing procedures. It consisted of an enema and a hot bath with cayenne, mustard, and ginger powder. You sink into this bath for at least 15 minutes, drink a lot of herbal tea and then someone wraps you in a cold sheet soaked in a bucket of ice and lies you down in bed for at least three hours—and in fact lying there the entire night would be even better. This procedure was meant to induce an artificial fever, known as hyperthermia. During this time, your immune system kicks in and your body produces more white blood cells.

This process, called leukotaxis, doubled the speed of white blood cells for every degree over the normal 98.6F. For example, if your body reaches a temperature of 103 degrees, white blood cells move 16 times faster. This procedure also draws out old poisons from your body, and due to its intensity can bring out buried emotional trauma in a way that some people begin to cry or scream. I was doing a weekly cold-sheet treatment, lying in the bath for 20 to 30 minutes with no emotions at all … while my temperature increased to 100.4F.

We could trace my progress by my condition, my blood test results (which I had before each treatment) and the shrinking of the size of the tumor. I'd already received two months of chemotherapy and I remained mostly on fresh juices, herbs, and Dr. Schulze's super food, feeling full from the amount of liquid I was drinking. My weight was stable. I had some weakness, chills, and nausea but still found the strength to continue the program. My blood tests showed perfectly stable liver and kidney function, along with electrolytes and protein. My blood cells were dropping due to the chemotherapy poison. I was trying to manage my anemia (low red blood cells) with fresh carrot, beetroot and green juices, along with super food (which contains a lot of protein too) and flavins. The cold-sheet treatment helped me to bring my lymphocytes up.

According to my oncologist, my response to the first course of two months of chemo was "tremendous" and the tumor shrank to 2.5 by 2 cm by palpation (from being 9.3 cm by 3.5 initially). I could see huge progress in my condition, and at that time I realized that after the next three months and the second regimen of chemotherapy, I would be free from cancer if I continued to do what I was doing.

Now I felt I needed a break, and so we left for Canada for a few days.

CHAPTER FOUR:

Raising Consciousness

"No problem can be solved from the same level of consciousness that created it."
—Albert Einstein

I t was good to be at home with my family. I felt better, more energized, emotionally and physically stronger, and ready for my second course of treatment. We came back from Canada on June 3rd and I had the opportunity to be at residency graduation party. It was great to see everyone and express my thanks in person. I can't emphasize enough the importance of my residency support and care during my disease.

On June 6th 2011, they started me on a new regimen of chemotherapy, one that I was supposed to receive for the next three months, with follow-up surgery, radiation, and continued chemotherapy for the next seven months.

My parents were coming from Kazakhstan to stay with me and take care of me, since my husband had to go back to work in Canada. I was supposed to be the one taking care of them, and now it was the other way around—at least temporarily. They were always helping us, though: giving us the best they could, and seeing the meaning of their life in our lives.

During my residency I'd been impatient to bring them to Canada, to surround them with love and give them everything they'd ever dreamed about. Their well-being concerned me, and I needed to get well to be able to take care of them during their later years. I felt responsible, wanted to finish my residency as soon as possible, and start working again.

I was the younger daughter and news about my disease was so hard for my mother that she couldn't stop crying, not being able to be next to me at this crucial moment. It seemed that everything we'd planned was crashing and nobody knew how it would turn out for any of us now. I called her every day, trying to calm her down and lift her spirits. She asked about my chemotherapy, my appetite - all the things mothers usually ask their children.

Although we were very close to each other, I didn't know how to tell her about Dr. Schulze's program and the fact that I was staying mostly on a juice and vegan diet while on chemotherapy. It sounded like such nonsense! I also knew that Dr. Schulze would never support me in this approach, but I just chose to blindly follow my soul, and it didn't matter to me how illogical my decision seemed and what others might say about it.

The deep feeling of *knowledge* that I was healthy was rooted inside me and strengthened my belief in what I was doing. I understood that my mother was neither emotionally nor psychologically ready for this, since it was hard to comprehend and value, especially in the rigid mind of a medical doctor. But I knew that soon somehow I would have to tell her about it.

It was obvious that many people around me believed strongly in the standard protocol regimen and resisted alternative medicine. And the reality is that I was exactly the same as them - until I embarked on my own journey.

Indeed, I had a cancer patient in a neighborhood clinic who refused to follow traditional medicine. I thought that he had no chance of surviving, and I was trying hard to convince him to change his mind.

Two sides of a great divide, and where was the truth?

I was a medical doctor surrounded by other medical doctors and the best medicine in the world, but now, in spite all of this, through the eyes of my soul, I knew that there was something beyond our logical mind and I needed to find it. I turned to the questions that continued to pop up again and again in my head. *Why I am searching for love, and what is hidden behind it for me? Why did I have to be so seriously sick to find this answer? How is it that some people heal, but others don't? What is the true meaning of body-mind-spirit interconnection and what role does it play in our life? Why is my perception of the disease so different from others', with no fear of death?*

I also couldn't explain why I was so convinced that I was healthy. I just knew it. My belief gave me strength, confidence, and the courage that I could inspire people who were close to me, with my attitude and behavior and give them hope for my well-being.

I felt more comfortable being isolated from society's edicts. I didn't particularly want to participate in any support groups or meetings devoted to cancer. From my point of view, they were focusing on the *problem*, talking about cancer and fighting with it instead of accepting and loving it by understanding its message and focusing on health. I wasn't *against* these groups and could see their value, but now being a cancer patient, I wanted to take a different approach.

You can't beat your enemy if you can't read his/her mind—or at least sit at the round table of negotiation. For ages, people have been fighting cancer using science's logical mind, and yet they were powerless. Why do we still use the same weapon, the same standard approach, just making it more and more advanced? Why can't we admit the existence of "something" that we may not yet be able to explain, and try to find the answer by going beyond our minds, following our hearts and souls?

How could I explain to my colleagues what my soul was telling me while on the other side of the fence?

It was hard to explain what I felt, even to people who were close to me, and I was aware that until I was able to bring all the puzzles together, nobody would understand me.

So I shut up and didn't talk about it beyond my family circle.

CHAPTER FIVE:

A Search for Answers

"If you don't believe it, you won't understand it."
—Saint Augustine

My new regimen of chemotherapy (using Herceptin and Tamoxifen) was supposed to be easier than the previous one, but it wasn't really: it strongly impacted my emotional state. The new drugs influenced my hormonal status, causing mood swings (which made me cry easily without reason) and in addition my eyes became watery—I shed tears all the time and it looked like I was crying, even I was not. My nails began to turn black. The drugs were taking control of my emotions, making me behave like a grouchy baby.

I felt powerless, even though I knew the reason for my condition; it was horrible not being able to do anything about it. I became sensitive to and picky about everything around me, and there were days when I cried just because I was in the "mood" to cry. It was bizarre and so outside of my usual strong optimistic personality: I was an athletic and healthy person, and I just couldn't relate to this. Even during my residency, after long hard shifts, when I felt overwhelmed and exhausted, I'd drive from the hospital to a nearby trail for rollerblading to restore myself physically and mentally surrounded by Mother Nature. Now, during my morning marathon to the lake after finishing yoga, I tried to do some jogging, but my legs didn't listen to me and I quickly became breathless. Besides, there was a weird correlation between jogging and tears: the faster I began to walk, the more I cried, and it was driving me nuts.

In spite of all this, I followed Dr. Schulz's program strictly, telling everybody in my family that they had to be patient and just believe in me.

The more I read books and information on different cancer treatment methods and stories of those who could heal, the more I became aware that the reason cancer still remains an incurable disease is because something is hidden behind the comprehension of our logical mind, something that our consciousness is not ready to admit yet and science can't prove.

If there are natural phenomenon like black holes, miracles, and other paranormal occurrences that science can't explain, it means that you may find the answer only if you allow yourself to think 'outside the box' of a logical mind and be open to ideas and theories which might not make any sense to you now. It's very hard for the mind to admit this, since we're all trained and programmed to behave and think in the pattern of a standard protocol to fit in society's framework.

We are held so tightly by obligations, finances, responsibilities, and duties that we can rarely afford to step out of the box and allow our souls to fly with our dreams. We are fearful, and it feels safer for us to cover our ears, screw up our eyes, and ignore those inner voices. But when you are on the other side of the fence, facing death, you have to make your choice: either live in fear and die during cancer's forced march, or follow your heart and fly with your soul.

At that point I began to wonder which chakras (centres of Prana, life force, or vital energy) were involved in breast cancer patients, since I wanted to look at the situation from an energy-blockage perspective. I was really fascinated by acupuncture, which I'd studied and practiced in

Kazakhstan. The eastern philosophy of understanding the human body/ organ functioning differs from the western approach and is based on the theory of Yin and Yang energy distribution (the life force that vitalizes all life forms) through chakras and meridians in the human body.

The main idea is that our bodies have seven chakras and fourteen principal meridians. The chakras represent concentrated energy centers, or pumps, projected in one of the seven points from the base of your spine to the top of your head, through which there is a connection with a universal source of energy. The role of the chakras is to bathe the organs in their energy, while the meridians' role is to deliver that energy to the organs. Meridians nourish all our organs with energy, including every physiological system (immune, nervous, respiratory, digestive, endocrine, circulatory, lymphatic, muscular and skeletal).

If a meridian's energy is blocked or disrupted, the system it feeds will be jeopardized. All meridians are connected with the surface of the skin through hundreds of tiny reservoirs of heat called acupuncture points, which can be stimulated with needles for energy distribution during acupuncture. The energy flow is affected by daily/seasonal cycles of nature, our emotions and thoughts, and strictly regulated by time and order - going from one meridian to another only at a certain time.

While practicing acupuncture in Kazakhstan I always talked to my patients, wanting to find out *where* the energy blockage was. It was like a puzzle, like doing math, when through a patient's complaints I managed to identify "fullness" or "emptiness" of certain channels and then move the energy in the right direction.

Usually I saw neurology patients in the clinic from nine to five, then went to my private office to work as an acupuncturist, where I managed patients with multiple complaints sent to me by different specialists. I could help patients with back pain and coughing so well that after one or two sessions they were symptom-free. I attributed my success to a deep understanding of the main principles of energy flow for these particular cases, since I knew exactly what I was doing with it.

I remember a woman who came to me with a diagnosis of chronic bronchitis and persistent dry cough for four months. She told me she'd tried everything, but without much relief, and now felt depressed and exhausted. She hadn't slept well for months, and today her co-workers couldn't stand her cough anymore and let her leave work early to do something about it.

She was coughing the whole time we talked.

She was asking for help and I saw it as straightforward. Within 10 minutes of the acupuncture treatment she stopped coughing and fell asleep, snoring deeply. I thought about waking her, since other patients were being treated in the same room. What was amazing was that everybody who heard her story asked me to let her rest. It seemed that every patient in the room wanted to safeguard her sleep. When the session was over, she felt much better, and during the next two sessions her cough left her completely.

So I knew from my own experience that patients can heal when you activate and restore their natural healing energies. I had many other acupuncture stories with positive outcomes, and now I was trying to look at cancer from that same energy-blockage point of view. I thought that if I knew which chakras were involved in breast-cancer patients, and what had led to this blockage, I could at least try to restore some balance.

Through my search I found out that breast and lung cancer were associated with blockages in the fourth chakra. The fourth chakra is located in our heart center and represents an emotional zone. It is a center of love, intuition, harmony, and forgiveness. A blocked capacity to fully express and resolve your feelings—anger, hostility, love, grief, joy and forgiveness—can block energy in the fourth chakra. This chakra takes care of the balance of giving and receiving; it's about the nurturing of self, versus the nurturing of others - in other words, the inability to love yourself, while mothering the whole world. Physical dysfunctions caused by blockage of the fourth chakra include breast cancer, heart attacks, lung cancer, chest pain, congestive heart failure, hypertension, asthma, allergies, pneumonia, upper back and shoulder problems.

After looking through all this information, I realized that on my journey the key to healing my cancer would depend on my capacity to release emotional pain through forgiveness of myself/others, and understand what the true meaning of love is: self-love versus self-appreciation, unconditional love and love toward others.

It seemed I couldn't escape from these questions and although I was reading all the books I'd bought about love, I still couldn't comprehend what I was missing, since nothing was new for me. I lived my life like everybody else, had my family and lovely parents. I loved and was loved: *what do I need to discover for myself, and where is the answer?*

I continued my treatment along with an intensive program of detoxification, persistent meditation with yoga, and remained on a juice/vegan diet. I felt weak, was emotionally vulnerable, but otherwise had almost no physical complaints. All of my blood tests—along with diagnostic heart imaging—showed that my organs were functioning normally and my tumor was shrinking rapidly. My parents were arriving in a week via Michigan where they'd flown to see Irina first, as she was dealing with their invitation papers. It was time for me to tell my mother about the Dr. Schulze program, to give her time to digest the information and prepare herself psychologically.

When I told her about my juice/vegan diet while being on chemotherapy she became upset. "How can a medical doctor do this? Where will you get your protein if you don't eat meat or milk products?" But she calmed down once she saw my positive results. Every day on the phone she begged me not to stop chemotherapy, and I promised. I told her how good Dr. Schulze's program was and that she needed to try it, too, but she didn't want to hear.

It had been almost two months since I'd started the program, and I could see the amazing results. I knew it was working. I also acknowledged the fact that chemotherapy was in fact playing a significant role in the shrinkage of the tumor as well. I badly needed my mother to be next to me with her love and support; but how could I make her trust in my belief, in what I was doing? How could I make her look at the world of cancer through the eyes of a daughter following her soul in hope of finding the way out?

I didn't know what to do. I knew one thing for sure: that she would follow me everywhere. If she needed to jump off a cliff for me in order to save my life, she'd do so without a moment's hesitation. I didn't see any way to convince her of the importance of what I was doing, other than letting her immerse herself in the program and experience it fully.

So I came up with a plan and bought a package of Dr. Schulze's "incurable disease" program for her without letting her know. I felt that she needed to go through it and be with me in the same boat, otherwise she'd continue to doubt it by attributing all my positive results only to the chemotherapy and not be able to hear what I was trying to say about the rest of it. I also thought it would benefit both of us in many different ways: she would experience first hand the effectiveness of the program and improve her health, while the program would keep her busy and away from all her worries and fears; and she would follow me and become my companion.

By now my parents were busy tasting the American lifestyle, spending time with Irina and her family, eating everything they wanted, drinking, and enjoying a social life. My dear mother: she was unaware that she was about to be exposed to an intensive body, mind and spirit washing-out detoxification program while visiting her little daughter!

CHAPTER SIX:

My Parents' Journey

*"A journey of a thousand miles must begin
with a single step."*
—Lao Tzu

W hen my parents arrived and I revealed my surprise to my mother, she didn't have any choice but to agree to join me on Dr. Schulze's program. In the past when I'd told her about healthy vegetarian diets, she'd always asked me to leave her alone. This time, she was ready to make a heroic sacrifice for her daughter, and I was grateful.

We decided that she would join me after one week of adaptation to her new place. Like most elderly people she took pills for high blood pressure, cholesterol, and diabetes. She tried to follow some diets, but couldn't resist eating meat and all the yummy things that make you feel good. The main ingredient of the national cuisine in Kazakhstan is meat and Kazakh dishes (like *bishparmak, manty, kazy*) are very delicious. Once you try it, it's hard to become vegetarian, especially if you cook it at home for your family!

On the other hand, there are more limited vegetables and greens there, especially in winter, so the diet of the majority of people consists of meat, potatoes, noodles, rice, and some vegetables.

Nevertheless, nearly all products are natural and very tasty - "organic" as we'd say in the US - because they don't use pesticides, antibiotics or hormones.

It was my parents' first trip to the US and everything was new, interesting, and exciting. The whole world here seemed different: people, culture, mentality, language, lifestyle, stores, food, and even nature. My mother, who was known for her open, optimistic and generous personality, could easily "talk" to people with her hands without knowing the language. She was touched by people's kindness and hospitality, since everybody was ready to explain and help with whatever question she had. Sometimes, when she wanted to maintain a conversation, she asked me to translate and I was amazed by her ability to joke, laugh, and hug people she'd just met. My father enjoyed everything quietly and spent his free time reading the Bible.

During the first week of living with us my mother began to accompany me to chemotherapy and witness my program first hand. Since I remained physically active and could manage my condition without difficulties, she watched me with curiosity and tried to help with whatever I was doing. The only part of the program we didn't let her participate in was the cold-sheet treatment. She just couldn't see me going through this "torture" and cried silently every time my husband soaked me in the hot bath with cayenne, mustard, and ginger powder. When I tried to tell her that cancer was just a message of love for me and I was healthy, she hugged me with tears in her eyes and begged me to continue chemotherapy.

After staying for a few days with my parents, my husband left for his work in Canada. Now, having observed me on Dr. Schulze's program, my mother was ready to step into it. My day started at six o'clock with a trip to the lake, and my dear elderly parents expressed a desire to accompany me.

Every day we got up early and drove to the lake, where I practiced yoga and meditation, while they both enjoyed the nature, walking in the park, picking mushrooms, or sitting on the bench near the lake. They believed in me! I could feel their love, support, and willingness to "jump of the cliff" if needed. We were a team now and I realized that it wasn't just my journey any more, but a trial for all the people who were close to me.

A trial for love ...

Since the program was very intensive, we stayed busy and didn't have time for any negative thoughts, feelings, worries or fears. We tried to enjoy as much as we could by being together in the present moment, putting all our energy into the program and building up my health. Now we were able to trace my mother's progress by checking her blood pressure and blood glucose level every day. After being on the program for a week she felt much better and even stopped taking pills for her blood pressure, since it had stabilized and come back into the normal range.

Later, we also reduced her diabetes pills from three to one a day, as her blood glucose was going down. Although it was very difficult for her to be on a juice/vegan diet and she was still craving meat, she managed to stay away from it while still cooking it for my father. I could see her excitement from the results of the program and the changes in her awareness. We had become true companions on our journey.

Four months had passed since I started chemotherapy and I'd been on Dr. Schulze's program for three of them. My tumor was shrinking rapidly, and my oncologist couldn't detect it anymore through physical examination (by palpation). In a month, by the end of the second course of chemotherapy, we were planning to do a follow-up MRI of the breast. Afterward, according to standard protocol, I was supposed to go through surgery, radiation, and seven months of chemotherapy no matter what the MRI results might be.

It was time for me to take the next step, to make a profoundly life-changing choice.

Would I follow the standard protocol or continue my journey following my soul and searching for an answer to why I had to face the cancer to find out what love is?

Why does the standard protocol require a person to go through chemo, surgery, and radiation if the MRI doesn't show any traces of tumor? Because an MRI can't detect the smallest cancer cells, which can still be there?

So we poison, burn, and cut it off? But doesn't experience show that we have been doing this for ages and it hasn't worked? If the body-mind-spirit is one whole entity, where all three elements are connected and influence and depend on each other, why do we repeatedly use the same approach of burning, cutting, and poisoning the physical body (one part of the whole) but ignore the other two?

Why do we continue to treat the physical body, making our weapons more advanced, and still hoping that it will work? What roles do the mind and spirit play in people's well-being that we don't yet know and/or can't accept? Do we resist admitting miracles of healing because we can't prove it with science?

But even if we can't explain it with science now, it doesn't mean that it does not exist.

What if the perception of our world, which we imbibed with our mother's milk - with all its beliefs, attitudes and dogmas - set up frames of limitations for us, and we can't explain miracles because they don't fit into this frame? Why do I feel so different from others, having a strong conviction that I am healthy and not afraid of death? Why so deep inside me is there a knowledge that I need to complete this journey to find what love is? What weird things! Where is the answer?

I continued my search by reading books, listening to CDs, participating in online conferences, praying, meditating, doing yoga, detoxifying … but again … and again … and again there was so much information on letting go, realizing, forgiving, positive affirmations, detoxification, diet, meditation—but I couldn't find the answer to the questions I had.

It was time for my parents to go back to Michigan and then fly home to Kazakhstan.

My husband was coming from Canada to stay with me for another three weeks. I could see the huge progress in my mother's condition after being on Dr. Schulze incurable program. After doing it for a month, she'd expressed a desire to continue for two more weeks with me. Now she'd fallen in love with the program and a vegetarian diet, she felt more energized, was taking only one pill, had a good blood-pressure reading and stable blood sugar in the normal range. She had stopped crying and her perception of the world had changed. Now she was supporting me in most of my decisions.

CHAPTER SEVEN:

The Soul's Rebellion

*"People will do anything, no matter how absurd,
to avoid facing their own soul. One does not
become enlightened by imagining figures of light,
but by making the darkness conscious."*
—Carl Gustav Jung

During this time my physical condition remained the same, with only one exception: my nails turned black, the nail beds became inflamed, and pus came out of them all the time.

I felt a growing protest inside myself. My every cell, my heart, my soul were all telling me that I needed to believe in myself and go my own way to see what was behind the framework that our perception doesn't allow us to accept. I had only three chemotherapy treatments left and couldn't wait for them to be over.

Usually I tolerated my chemotherapy sessions well and could stay active after them. But this time when we came home from a regular treatment, I felt so weak that I had to go to bed. For the first time I had the feeling that I was dying. I didn't have any fear of death, and felt indifferent toward everything: my soul and heart were giving up. When I closed my eyes I clearly saw a picture of a cemetery with a big field of scorched grass behind it. I was standing in the field, looking around, and couldn't see any life, just the cemetery nearby.

Right away I had a feeling that this scorched field was associated with me. This was exactly how I felt! The chemotherapy had "burned" me inside out; symbolically, I was a burned field with no life. I was standing there looking at the cemetery and not knowing where to go and what to do. My soul and heart were crying.

When I opened my eyes, I knew it was a message for me: if I continued the standard treatment, I would end up in that cemetery. My soul was telling me that my path was different. *But where it is? In what direction do I need to go to find the answers to my questions? What is hidden behind this?*

In the past I had answers to my questions through pictures suddenly coming through, and I trusted my intuition. Since I had only one chemo session left, I decided to skip it and go for an MRI.

I had an MRI of the breast on August 25, 2011 that showed complete resolution of the previously noted left-breast tumor, along with no metastases in the lymph nodes under my arm, though there were still some residuals in the breast tissue. A six-month follow-up was recommended. This news was a big relief, although I clearly realized that despite no sign of a tumor on the MRI, it could come back at any time and this didn't mean *I had made a* complete recovery.

I understood that staying free from cancer in the future could only happen if my healing journey of body-mind-spirit were to continue and I could find the answers to all my questions. And now I had even more questions! *What does complete healing mean? In what cases does cancer come back?*

During this time I tried to talk to some of my colleagues and get their opinions on my situation, but mostly I felt pressure to continue the official treatment regimen. My soul protested and I wanted to escape from it. *If there are no clinical trials done for groups of women who had complete resolution of breast tumor with follow-up surgery, radiation, and chemo, versus those who didn't go through it, why do we consider the standard protocol the best if we don't know the outcomes of those who don't undergo it? If none of these approaches gives a guarantee, what is the point of this torture? It may give you more years to live, but what is the quality of this life?*

I still hesitated about what my next step should be. I had a few months left to finish the residency, but I knew that while feeling burned and empty inside I couldn't give anything—not to my patients, and not to myself. I needed time to restore myself physically, mentally and emotionally. I thought of how embarrassing it would be for patients to see a doctor standing in front of them with inflamed fingernails and tears flowing down her cheeks.

Because of his work situation, my husband couldn't stay any longer and had to go back to Canada. I felt that being alone was going to be very hard for me now. Besides, this experience and being on the other side of the medical fence made me think and feel differently. My feelings and thoughts seemed totally absurd, even to me, when I looked at it through the prism of a logical mind. Having the strong conviction of being healthy inside, and knowing that this was my journey to find the meaning of love, I didn't want to be exposed to the external World truth where everybody would now see and treat me as a cancer patient and wouldn't be able to understand me.

I wanted to hide from this world, dive within, follow my soul and keep my belief within me as an anchor to life. What would I say to others? I felt I had only one way to go: I decided to withdraw from the residency with the option of returning within the next two years.

Looking back, I see that I wouldn't have been able to do what I did without being in the residency. All that experience and knowledge was incredibly valuable for my inner growth and recovery. I truly believe that my residency program was one of the best residencies: it not only gave me knowledge, but also tremendous support during my disease. I was part of it and it was part of me. I was provided with guidance and support whenever I needed it. I felt enormous gratitude towards my program director, as he always had the patience to listen to me and keep an open mind without bias when my situation was discussed.

But now I felt I had to continue treatment in Canada, staying there with my family: it was not a time to be alone.

Meanwhile, I made an appointment with the oncologist in Toronto and had the chance to get one more chemotherapy treatment with Herceptin while I was here. In clinical trials, this drug had shown very promising results and was considered best for women who had tested positive for HER2. I had already finished two courses of chemo and was supposed to receive a loading dose of Herceptin before the third course.

I didn't know what to do. I felt exhausted from five months of chemotherapy and the inner battle between my mind and heart, to the extent that I just wanted to have a break and make a decision about my next step.

My mother was calling and begging me again to get it done, since clinical trials showed that Herceptin reduces the chances of breast cancer coming back or spreading; and I agreed to have one more treatment. My soul was rebelling, telling me that I was ignoring the message, while my heart protested that I was making my decision following the mind, with no answer for Love there...

PART II:

Opening the Heart

CHAPTER EIGHT:

Looking Inside the Pain

"There is no coming to consciousness
without pain."
—Carl Gustav Jung

A fter I received chemo and we came home, I felt very sick and began experiencing severe stomach pain. It was a new symptom that I hadn't had before, and I didn't know what it could mean. The next day, my pain didn't go away. It was alleviated for a couple of hours after eating or taking medication, but then came back. I'd felt much better when I was going through chemotherapy than I did now. The pain woke me every night and it seemed I couldn't escape from it. Often, when medication or food didn't help, I squatted in the darkness of the night wondering what direction I should go in.

Why didn't I follow my heart, if I felt that a picture of scorched grass with a cemetery was a message from my soul? Is this stomach pain a warning sign for me? Why is there a duality in what I feel with my heart and what I do? Because what

I feel isn't logical and is weird for the mind? Because society/environment/families have established rules, dogmas and principles that limit your mind and program you to think in a certain pattern—and you are stuck there?

Where does this belief that I am healthy coming from? If it is coming from the soul, does it mean that my soul knows something and is trying to convey it to me? Does this stomach pain mean that I'm trying to deny all my feelings? Does it mean that if I continue to ignore it and follow the standard protocol, I will betray myself and end up at the cemetery?

Now I was remembering a story. Three months before I was diagnosed with cancer, I had a phone consultation with the well-known Australian astrologist, Lynda Hill. At that time I was applying for jobs in the US and Canada and was curious as to which direction I needed to take. What she told me came as a great surprise. She said, "You shouldn't work as a medical doctor; your soul came to this earth with a mission and you need to accomplish it. You're like a monk who will come down from the mountains and bring an important message to people."

When I asked her what message it was, she responded, "you'll bring knowledge from an ancient time that people forgot about."

"So if I don't work as a medical doctor, what will I do?" I asked.

"You will write a book," she said, "but it will be about health, not medicine."

I didn't know what to think about that conversation. It seemed to be nonsense: I was applying for jobs, I didn't have any messages for anyone and I wasn't going to write any book. Moreover, when three months later I found I had a stage-three cancer, I was frustrated that it hadn't shown up in the astrology reading.

Now, looking back, I found many strange aspects to my story. I doubted astrology reading at that time but my mammogram didn't show a 10-centimeter tumor, either. Based on the standard approach, breast tissue is considered dense until a woman is 35 years old, so mammograms aren't done before then. *How dense does it have to be in a 47-year-old woman in order to hide a huge tumor? Why did I have this strong conviction that I was healthy?*

But for now I was just suffering from pain and didn't have any answers.

The pain had the clinical presentation of a duodenal ulcer (which was later confirmed by gastro-endoscopy). I stopped taking blood-thinner pills and went to see my oncologist in Toronto who told me that I needed to go with the standard protocol and continue chemotherapy.

When I told him that I wanted to stay away from it, he said that the cancer would come back if I didn't and that I wouldn't stand a chance. He scheduled another appointment to give me time to think and do something about the pain. Before scheduling a follow-up breast MRI, it was mandatory to have another mammogram. If a mammogram couldn't identify a 10-centimeter tumor, what could it show now? Why not to go with an ultrasound and an MRI? Clinical studies have shown that ultrasounds detect three to four additional cancers per 1,000 women with dense breasts that mammograms miss. *We put so much effort and money into breast cancer awareness campaigns, why couldn't we establish a standard regulation for every state/country to follow up with ultrasound for those women with dense breast tissue to pick it up in the early stages?*

I continued to be involved in a healing program, trying to do everything possible (and impossible!) at the physical, mental, and spiritual levels: staying on a juice/vegan organic diet, doing yoga, meditation, chanting, taking infrared sauna with sound and light therapy, singing, taking hot/cold shower, doing skin brushing, visualization, affirmations, praying, reading books, participating in online conferences, and doing further research on body-mind-spirit interconnection ... but my condition remained.

In fact, within three weeks I began experiencing a new acute pain in different parts of my body, which I'd never had before - right shoulder, left side of the belly, - which allowed me to lie in bed only in a certain position, since any movement caused pain. It was bizarre. All my blood tests, abdominal ultrasounds, and physical exams were normal: it wasn't clear what it could be.

CHAPTER NINE:

Confession

"The heart that breaks open can contain the whole universe... All is registered in the 'boundless heart' of the Bodhisattva. Through our deepest and innermost responses to our world – to hunger and torture and the threat of annihilation – we touch that boundless heart."
—Joanna Macy

One of those days after meditation, I found myself sitting and crying and repeating all the time: "I want to go back home, I want to go home."

It was so unexpected to be perplexed, but I could feel right away that it was a cry from my soul. Somewhere deep inside I knew that I was trying to have it both ways: not being able to fully rely on my heart's decisions and follow my soul. My logical mind was standing in the way of every thought and feeling coming from my heart, constantly doubting it if it didn't fit into the comprehension-niche.

Still, it was difficult for my mind to accept the absurdity of my feelings of being healthy while suffering from pain and looking for an answer hidden behind the love. I realized that what I was doing all this time was negotiating between my mind and my heart, trying to find a compromise: doing chemotherapy and Dr. Schulze's healing program at the same time, taking a break from the residency to continue treatment but resisting going for chemo, surgery, and radiation.

I was involved in an intensive healing program and was trying to find the answers to my questions, but at the same time the logical mind of a medical doctor was clinging on to its privilege of being dominant and didn't want to destroy my established belief system. The battle between my mind and heart continued. I didn't have the courage to go into free-flight with my soul, I'd ignored its message … and now it seemed that my soul wanted to give up.

How often do we hide or ignore what we feel in our souls, finding thousands of excuses and following standard behavior patterns, because of our fear of seeing the truth and making changes in our lives? Changes are painful because they bring fear of uncertainty—and we often choose what is more comfortable, feeling safe and protected. We feel safe in the prison of our mind and don't want to hear anything that could shake our convictions.

After this episode, I promised myself to follow my soul and make decisions from my heart, until I could find the answers to all my questions.

I stepped into uncertainty, ready for change.

It's odd: I would never have believed someone telling me that I wouldn't choose to follow the full range of standard medical protocols, especially since I had access to the best medicine in the world. I declined follow-up chemo, surgery, and radiation, because I felt that it wasn't my way, and that this approach would terminate me sooner than the cancer: for me, it was a fast track to oblivion.

I also stopped taking pain-relief medication since it wasn't helping me.

Now, as always when facing a challenge, I accepted my pain with gratitude, trying to look at it as a messenger, to listen and understand what my heart was telling me. In our metaphysical world, modern medicine views the physical body (a human being) as the only dimension of our existence, mainly controlled by the brain. Contrary to this view, natural healing (at the body-mind-spirit level) considers every human being not just as a physical body, but as a multi-dimensional living being, dependent upon a life force energy (called Chi, or Prana, or Qi) that runs through the body's meridian system and connects to the universal source.

The fact that matter/mass is a very concentrated form of energy was proven by Albert Einstein in 1925 with his famous equation $E=MC2$ (where E =total energy, M = mass/or matter, C= speed of light in a vacuum, squared). It means that energy and matter are the same things, only in different forms.

In other words, everything is energy!

Before this discovery, based on Isaac Newton's theory, it was believed that the universe was made of atoms (solid objects), attracted to each other by gravity. What Einstein's discovery proved was that those atoms could be broken down into subatomic particles, and due to their high rate of vibration, create the appearance of solidity, yet at their core they are comprised of pure energy.

If our body/matter is a concentrated form of energy (chi) that runs through chakras and meridians, nourishes all our organs and systems, and connects our body with our consciousness (spirit) through the chakras, then healing cancer can occur only if we see ourselves as multi-dimensional beings at the body-mind-spirit level. To accept this means to admit our connection with the universal source. *Then, if this is true and we are not just our physical bodies, but the whole unity of three elements (body-mind-spirit) why do we expect to cure ourselves of cancer by just treating the physical body? Is this a reason why our approach with standard protocols has never worked? If we have a connection with the universal source, then what universal laws does the body-mind-spirit obey? What is the relationship and interconnection between them? Does it mean we can heal if we follow these laws?*

I wanted to see the whole picture.

CHAPTER TEN:

Your Body's Energy System

"Our scientific power has outrun our spiritual power. We have guided missiles and misguided men."
—Dr. Martin Luther King, Jr.

B ased on the eastern approach to the functioning of the human body, health means having a free and balanced energy flow, which can be affected by many factors—including our thoughts and emotions.

All our emotions have a direct impact on our physical health and are associated with different parts of the body. For example, liver problems are associated with anger, headaches with negative thinking, heart problems are connected to our relations with our partner (when we can't accept her/him the way she/he is); the stomach is responsible for deep offense, low self-esteem, and leaking energy from there (the third chakra) while looking for approval; kidney problems are always connected with offenses and pretensions to our family members. The left kidney is more associated with offenses toward others and the right kidney with dissatisfaction with yourself (self-realization) and so forth.

Nowadays we have many different techniques such as emotional-freedom techniques, releasing techniques, letting-go techniques and emotional-code techniques that are effective in releasing emotional pain. If you look through the literature related to cancer healing (or the healing of any disease) or if you get acquainted with programs at retreat centers for cancer patients or talk to those who have healed, you'll see that a very important part of the healing process is letting go of emotions and forgiving. This means releasing emotions (energy) blockages within the physical body and restoring their flow through meridians and chakras.

I was continuing my search through the literature, learning and practicing different "releasing" techniques, when Irina called me. "You have to put everything aside," she said excitedly, "and listen to Caroline Myss' audiobook on the energetics of healing". Caroline Myss is an American author of numerous books including five New York Times bestsellers; she's an internationally-recognized speaker in the field of human consciousness, spirituality, mysticism, health, energy medicine and medical intuition.

Over the past decade, her work with Norman Shealy, M.D., PhD, a Harvard-trained neurosurgeon and founder and first president of the American Holistic Medical Association, has shown a deep connection between emotional dysfunction and physical illness.

Since the idea of the chakras wasn't new for me, and I could see the positive effect of acupuncture (through energy distribution) while treating patients, it was very interesting to hear what this renowned western author would say about it. I was amazed by the depth of the energy-field exploration that Caroline Myss had done, and her ability to present very complex information in a simple and interesting way: I fell in love with her immediately.

She was not only showing the whole picture of our energy distribution throughout the chakras, pointing out its role and interconnection with the physical body, thoughts and emotions, but also describing the main reasons for energy blockages and leakages that can lead to health problems. She was giving the key points on how to disconnect this energy from past painful thoughts, emotions and memories and bring it back to the present time.[2]

Caroline Myss provides essential tools for personal evaluation and development by making us conscious of the hidden patterns in our behavior and the many issues to which we remain blind in our lives. She was the first person to convey knowledge on energy/chakras to a wider audience in such a way that anyone could begin the journey of self-discovery and love on their own and go through the process of deep transformation of personal awareness—just guided by her books and presentation.

---

[2] (watch her presentation online: http://www.youtube.com/watch?v=KckwhZE1NdY)

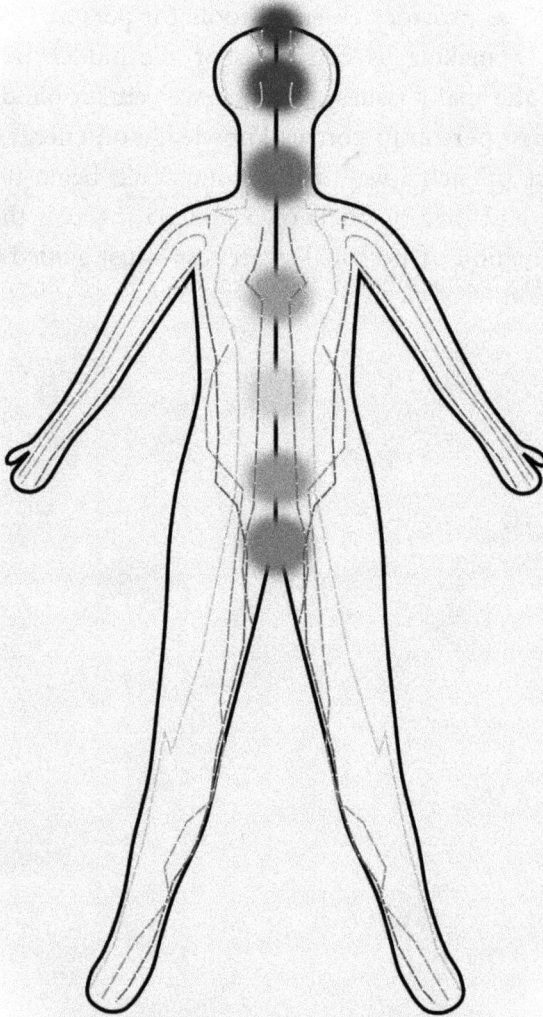

I recommend readers, especially those facing their own health challenges, to read Caroline Myss' original work themselves. Here is a brief description of the chakras.

The first chakra (root), lies at the bottom of the spine between the anus and the genitals and contains our belief patterns, attitudes, dogmas and group thought-forms, strongly connected to our biological family and impacted by the environment that surrounds us. It forms our perception (attitude, beliefs, judgment) and determines the choices we make in our life toward family, work/business and money. It represents how much trust and security we have.

Whatever "template" was "downloaded" to you will determine your life perception in these areas. Those who experienced childhood abuse or parental criticism and brought negative beliefs or attitudes like fear, anger or aggression into their lives can leak energy through connection with past memories or chakras may become blocked, clogged with stagnant energy, spin irregularly or backward. This can later lead to the development of physical body dysfunction in the organs supplied by this chakra such as the base of the spine, legs, bones, feet, rectum and the immune system. We can bring this energy back and restore the energy flow through forgiveness and letting go of these painful emotions and memories.

The second chakra (sacral) lies below the naval at the root of the genitals. It is a chakra of control, power distribution, and sexual relationships in our one–on–one interaction with others. This chakra is also responsible for creativity and friendship. We discharge energy when we try to control someone or allow others to control us; when we have addictions, feel guilty, aggressive, hostile, or continually dwell on memories of betrayal, physical violence, or sexual abuse. Physical body dysfunction related to this chakra is connected to the sexual organs— ovaries, testes; lower vertebra, bladder, large intestine, and hip area.

The third chakra corresponds to the solar plexus. This is a chakra of personal power, which is responsible for self-esteem, self-respect, confidence and honor. We leak energy from this chakra if we look for other people's approval, have decreased personal boundaries (afraid of making decisions, become manipulative), or have low self-esteem, confidence, or self-respect. These feelings and attitudes may cause disturbances in the energy flow and lead to gastric and duodenal ulcers, arthritis, pancreatitis, diabetes, liver dysfunction, hepatitis, intestinal problems with indigestion and kidney problems.

The fourth chakra lies in the middle of the chest, near the heart. It is our emotional zone and center for love: love of self, love of others. It is the center of self–acceptance and forgiveness. It is the generator of all our emotions: love and hatred, forgiveness and compassion, attachment, grief, anger, jealousy. When we experience painful/negative emotions and feel "drained" or exhausted, we are directing our energy into memories, situations or other people and losing it. Fourth chakra dysfunction will create energy blockages in the following organs: heart (heart attack, myocardial infarction, congestive heart failure, etc.), lungs (lung cancer, pneumonia, asthma), shoulders, upper back, arm, ribs, breast (breast cancer), and the thymus gland.

Caroline Myss describes fourth-chakra blockages as an inability to love yourself. She teaches "you have to have self-love in order to heal. Healing is a journey of forgiveness and understanding what love is. You have to discover who you are and begin your journey into a different quality of love. When you start this self-love journey you will change your physical location, and/or you will change your job, and/or you will change your relationship, because anything you built over this time is not going to make the transition over the river … and then you will change the way you look physically. When you go through the passage over the heart, you will discover the nature of the wounds and come to realization of why you have been hurt. Then you look at your whole life differently and that is why and where you discover the power of forgiveness. Loving yourself means listening to the messages that come from your heart and you have to have the courage to follow those feelings, since they will force you to change your life in any case. These messages often threaten the comfortably rational choices we have made with our heads."

This was exactly how I felt and what was going on in my life! Although I still couldn't fully understand the true meaning of love, or what is hidden behind it, I'd changed my physical location, left my job, and was struggling to follow my heart's messages. Indeed, I have a close friend in Kazakhstan who also had breast cancer and when I called her with excitement to tell her that I could help, she tried first, but then refused. When I asked her why, she began crying, telling me that she was "sitting in a tank" with tightly closed eyes and covered ears and couldn't see or hear me, because of her fear of change.

The fifth chakra lies in the throat region. It is the center of our will and choice. It is tied to our ability to speak up for ourselves and live the truth. This chakra imbalance leads to the following physical body dysfunctions: sore throat, thyroid problems, laryngitis, voice problems, mouth ulcers, gum and tooth problems, and scoliosis. To restore the function of the organs that are bathed by this chakra, we need to unplug our energy from the past and bring it to the present by learning to speak up for ourselves (have courage and honesty, never suppress feelings, have the will to describe our own needs) and establish our boundaries. We can also retrieve the energy through the act of confession. We need to have the desire to learn how to control ourselves (not others) by living the truth: that every thought we have and every choice we make has the power to bring change into our lives.

The sixth chakra lies between the eyebrows. It is the energy center that runs the mind. This chakra governs intuition and challenges us to look for illogical things, to find messages in coincidences, and to see beyond the rational and visible. Physical body dysfunctions caused by imbalance of this chakra include: brain tumors, hemorrhage, and strokes; blindness; deafness; neurological disturbances; seizures; and learning disabilities.

The seventh chakra is located at the top of the head. It is the center of our spiritual connections and our unity with the divine. Here we store and retrieve information from other realms. Seventh chakra dysfunction leads to life-threatening illness or accidents, skin disorders, and chronic exhaustion. The "dark night of the soul" experience is often related to this energy imbalance of this chakra.

The more I read and listened to Caroline Myss, the more I became aware that the only way for me to heal and find self-love was to go through a journey within, beyond the logical and rational mind and discover who I was. It seemed that heaven had sent me a teacher who was talking to me in a spiritual language and guiding me in my discovery.

I learned how to pray, how to follow the heart and investigate my attitudes, beliefs, and thoughts, so that I would know why I'd been hurt and so I could release these negative patterns. Now being at the other side of the fence, I had a soul companion and didn't feel lonely anymore. I was becoming more and more aware of my feelings and discovering a deep sense of something that initially seemed illogical and bizarre for the mind. My perception of the world was changing and I realized that I was the only one who was responsible for all the feelings and emotions I experienced.

CHAPTER ELEVEN:

Dr. Gerson's Protocol

"The human body is a machine which
winds its own springs."
—Julien Offroy de la Mettrie

To deal with a constant, annoying stomach (second to a duodenal ulcer) and abdominal pain (unclear etiology) which made me feel exhausted and wasn't letting me relax or do anything, I decided to endure the pain until I could investigate it from the inside out and see where my heart would guide me.

I thought that if I had feelings of being like a field of scorched grass, most likely this was what my digestive system looked like after chemotherapy. And just as a burned field of earth needs fertilizer, nutrients and water to produce a harvest, so a burned digestive system needs digestive enzymes to function properly and break down food.

Long before a patient develops cancer, he/she almost always has a weak, malfunctioning liver, and in many cases pancreatic insufficiency (decreased production of the pancreatic enzyme). In turn, chemotherapy destroys the digestive tract's healthy cells and worsens the condition even more.

So I decided to look at the role and importance of pancreatic enzymes in the body's defense mechanism against cancer.

The basic principle of digestive enzymes' function is the following: food digestion starts in our mouth by breaking down complex carbohydrates and lipids. The food then goes into the stomach, where it is broken down into amino acids by the gastric enzyme pepsinogen. Food then travels into the duodenum, where duodenal enzymes act as sensors and controllers between the stomach, the pancreas and the gallbladder. The pancreas produces lipase, amylase and protease, which split lipids, carbohydrates and proteins further.

Since cancer cells have a protein coating, the pancreatic proteolitic (protein-dissolving) enzyme can digest them, which makes the cancer cells vulnerable to immune cells. So if pancreatic enzyme production is impaired, cancer cells can hide from the immune system with a protein coating. When bile and pancreatic enzymes are secreted into the duodenum, duodenal enzymes regulate acidity, control activity and production of pancreatic juices and activate the contraction of the gall bladder to release pre-stored bile. If this complex digestive enzyme system isn't working properly—and is also burned by chemotherapy—what can pain medication do here, and how can cancer cells be destroyed?

The most important contribution in examining the role of pancreatic enzymes in cancer therapy was made by Scottish biologist Dr. John

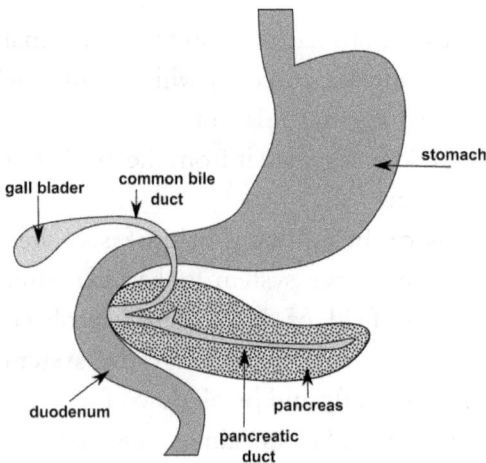

Beard. In 1906 he made several extraordinary observations and proposed that pancreatic proteolytic enzymes play an important role in the body's defense mechanism against cancer and may be useful as a cancer treatment.

He discovered that placenta (trophoblast) and cancer cells have a similar appearance and behavior - trophoblastic cells invade the uterus and reproduce its complex blood as cancer cells. Furthermore, he observed that on the 56th day of human pregnancy, the placenta stops growing and the fetus' pancreas begins to function. It brought him to the conclusion that the fetus' pancreas secreted something that stopped the growth of the placenta. Indeed, if the fetal placenta continues to grow, it leads to the development of a very aggressive cancer called choriocarcinoma.

Later on Beard would prove that pancreatic juices cause tumors to shrink: he injected juices extracted from young animals' pancreases into cancer tumors of both humans and animals. His work was published in the Journal of the American Medical Association (JAMA), and he wrote a book on enzyme therapy in cancer care.

After finding this information, I decided to look for evidence to see if pancreatic or any digestive enzymes had been used successfully in cancer patients, and what might be available on the market.

I felt that if I could "fertilize" my digestive system with enzymes, it would help me restore the function of my internal organs and lead to balance in my digestive system. Therefore I expected that the pain would eventually go away. Through the internet I found information about people who'd had cancer and were cured by taking raw pancreas and liver, but I was looking for evidence-based results from legal sources and wasn't convinced by this information.

Later, I discovered Max Gerson's therapy, which consists of diet, fresh juices, detoxification with a coffee enema, and supplements with minerals, vitamins, and digestive enzymes (made from bovine liver, with raw bovine and swine pancreas). Max Gerson (1881-1959) was a medical doctor who lived in the US and successfully treated patients with advanced cancer, TB, and chronic diseases. Nobel Prize laureate and former Gerson patient Albert Schweitzer said, "I see in Dr. Gerson one of the most eminent geniuses in the history of medicine." [3]

The main principle of his therapy was the concept that cancer patients have weakened immune systems and generalized tissue damage (especially in the liver) caused by the spread of toxic cancer products throughout the bloodstream. His program was demanding, intensive, and aiming to restore the whole organism, which then becomes able to heal itself. It consists of:

1. a strict vegan diet (high potassium, low sodium, with no fats or oils except flaxseed oil)

2. detoxification of the whole body with a coffee enema and hourly drinking freshly squeezed fruit and vegetable juices (the body's entire blood supply passes through the liver every three minutes, carrying toxins picked up from the body, which are released through the bile ducts. While the patient is holding a coffee enema in the colon for 12 to 15 minutes, it dilates the bile ducts and stimulates the excretion of toxic cancer cell breakdown products by the liver and dialysis of toxic products from the blood through the colon wall.

3. supplements of essential minerals and vitamins: potassium compound salt, niacin, B12, CoQ10, flaxseed oil and thyroid granules with lugol solution.

4. enzymes: injection of raw liver extract, liver capsules, pancreatin and acidol pepsin which are made of defatted bovine liver, raw bovine and swine pancreas.

Nowadays the Gerson Institute is run by Max Gerson's daughter Charlotte Gerson[4] and offers certified training programs for professionals, with practitioners all over the world.

I bought all the available books and discs of this program, studied, and decided to embark upon it. It was recommended to follow the

---

[3] http://gerson.org/gerpress/dr-max-gerson/
[4] (www.gerson.org)

program for up to two years (and even longer for patients who received chemotherapy). Although my MRI showed complete resolution of the tumor, I still had some residuals in the breast tissue that needed follow-up. I wanted to be on the safe side, since I still didn't have answers to my questions and was still in pain. I thought that this program would help me to relieve my stomach/abdominal pain by bringing my digestive enzymes into balance and restore health by cleansing my body of chemo and cancer cells.

The constant pain made me feel miserable and so I waited for the Gerson products impatiently. I remember the day when I received the package and took the first dose of liver and pancreas capsules: my stomach pain disappeared completely. Since that time I've never again experienced it and I've forgotten about my duodenal ulcer. It was like magic, and I couldn't believe that it was possible! Of course I expected pain relief, but not to that extent. I felt free from the pain and it seemed like a reward for listening to and following my heart. Now I could sleep at night and stay busy with the program during the day.

CHAPTER TWELVE:

The Black Swan

"It has been more profitable for us to bind together in the wrong direction than to be alone in the right one."
—Taleb Nassim Nikolas

I continued ordering books, reading, participating in online seminars, going to conferences, surrendering to God and asking for guidance, studying new meditation techniques, doing yoga, and looking for answers.

Since there were so many strange aspects of my journey and since all my attempts to explain my search for love embarrassed others, I isolated myself from the external world and completely immersed myself in my inner world, trying to listen to my heart and "go with the flow." You have to go through a rigorous transformation and it takes a great deal of fortitude to follow through with something that nobody else believes in.

It's an odd feeling when somebody tells you that you can't be healed, but you know through the eyes and perception of your soul ... that you can.

More and more often, when I asked for guidance in my prayers, I received information in images almost the next day. We ignore the fact that our higher self, which is connected to universal consciousness speaks to us in its own language of symbols, archetypes and metaphors. These symbols are the part of an ancient language we've forgotten. During meditation and prayers, when our mind reaches its quiet state, we become open to higher consciousness and can communicate with it and receive messages.

On one of these days, when I was doing a sound-healing meditation conducted by Dr. Mitchell Gaynor,[5] I suddenly saw a picture of two black swans. It was in the middle of the guided meditation when I was following an instruction on the imagery of light coming from the heart. My mind was immediately confused by this image and asked, perplexed: *what is it?*

The answer came right away: *it is you.*

I couldn't meditate any longer and wondered what this image could mean. *Why am I a black swan and what does this message mean to me?* I'd always had brown hair, although I'd become bald after chemotherapy, but nothing in my appearance could match this image. I shared the vision with Irina and Annie, asking for their help.

What we found was interesting.

The term "black swan" was originally a Latin expression. Its oldest reference was found in the work of Juvenal, a Roman poet of the late first and early second centuries, who wrote that "a good person is as rare as a black swan."[6] For many centuries, Europeans firmly believed that all swans were white, since nobody had seen a black one. All records reported that swans had white feathers.

---

[5] (medical oncologist, president of Gaynor Integrative Oncology in New York City and Assistant Clinical Professor of Medicine at Well-Cornell Medical College)

[6] *rara avis in terris nigroque simillima cygno.*

The "black swan" was a common expression in 16th century London used to describe an impossibility and was used in philosophical discussions of the improbable.

No one could have imagined that black swans might actually exist, until 1697, when one was discovered in Australia.

In 2007, Nassim Nicholas Taleb, author of the bestselling book *The Black Swan: The Impact of the Highly Improbable* was the first to use the term black swan as a metaphor. He wrote: "Before the discovery of Australia, people in the Old World were convinced that all swans were white, an unassailable belief as it seemed completely confirmed by empirical evidence. The sighting of a black swan might have been an interesting surprise for a few ornithologists (and others extremely concerned with the coloring of birds) but that is not where the significance of the story lies. It illustrates a severe limitation to our learning from observations and experience and the fragility of our knowledge. One single observation can invalidate a general statement derived from millennia of confirmed sightings of millions of white swans."[7]

He considers almost all major scientific discoveries, historical events and artistic accomplishments as "black swans", which are undirected and unpredicted.

Taleb notes that "what we call here a Black Swan (and capitalize it) is an event with the following three attributes. First, it is an outlier, as it lies outside the realm of regular expectations, because nothing in the past can convincingly point to its possibility. Second, it carries an extreme 'impact'. Third, in spite of its outlier status, human nature makes us concoct explanations for its occurrence after the fact, making it explainable and predictable. I stop and summarize the triplet: rarity, extreme 'impact,' and retrospective (though not prospective) predictability."

The main idea of the book is not so much to predict Black Swan events, but to be able to understand negative events and use positive ones. Taleb says that we always run the risk of experiencing the improbable,

---

[7] Taleb, Nassim Nicholas: *The Black Swan: The Impact of the Highly Improbable Fragility*, second edition.

rare and novel, and can either be shocked by this knowledge/experience … or we can be open to it. Black Swan events will happen whether we look for or anticipate them or not; it is up to us to find ways to integrate them into our lives and experiences.

Looking at a Black Swan totem,[8] I found that "The Black Swan lends a great capacity to open us up to the healing properties of love and happiness, and taking advantage of this at this current time will be very nourishing. The Black Swan can represent spiritual love and freedom."

This information resonated with me, since what I believed in and what looked weird and impossible for the whole world (i.e. that I was healthy and needed to embark on this journey to find the answer to the question of what love is) was true for me, and now I knew it was possible.

The symbol of the Black Swan suggested that what seemed impossible for the logical mind can be possible if you believe in it, listen to your inner self, and follow your heart. I felt that through the Black Swan symbol I received an explanation and support for my "weird" feelings, along with reassurance that I was on the right path. I also realized that a cure for cancer was possible - making the 'impossible' possible - and is to be found through the passage of love.

Now I wondered if a Black Swan might provide the path and whether it might help people open up to the healing power of love. *Is this the same message I need to deliver to people, the message that Lynda Hill was talking about in our consultation? But what exactly is so special about it? How did people forget its power? How can it cure cancer?*

I stayed on Dr. Gerson's therapy, continued my prayers, meditation, yoga, reading and finally the answer to my questions about love just came to me.

And it was …WOW…

---

[8] (http://moonvoice.dreamwidth.org/68137.html)

PART III:

The Healing Truth

CHAPTER THIRTEEN:
Finding the Love

"Love is the beauty of the soul."
—Saint Augustine

I came to the realization that my desperate search for true love was my unconscious search for myself, my infinite being, my true identity, which I'd lost. To find true love means to find your real self and to know who you are.

True love is a state of self, it is who we are, infinite beings: Love=Infinite being=soul=God= I=Divine= Light = Energy. Love is our inherent state, it is the true basic nature of our soul, but we have totally forgotten about it and remain asleep to the reality of this infinite state of being.

All the time, unconsciously, we are trying to return to this joyful inherent state by looking for love throughout our lives. But we can never find it. More and more often we hear from our masters and gurus that we are infinite perfect beings, but still can neither believe in it nor express

73

this infinite being. We can't accept it because for millions of years, while going through lifetimes, we have played a game of limitation. We have denied our true nature and lost connection with our inherent state of love so that it now seems illogical for our mind and takes extraordinary will for us to go in opposite direction to find it.

Everybody wants to love and be loved. We are all looking for love, in desperation, all our lives, and suffer if we don't have it. What does love mean for us? Where do we look for it? Why we can't find it?

We look for love from the day we're born. The newborn child needs mother's love to feel safe and secure, which means survival for him or her. When the child grows, he looks for love to feel protected and confident. Later on in our lives, we try to find happiness and joy by looking for a mate who will fit our parameters for the "ideal" partner and provide feelings of security (financial, emotional) and self-satisfaction (ego and sexual satisfaction).

Usually, in order to get what we want, we use a behavioral pattern called "gaining approval." We learned this pattern from our parents, learning to earn their love and feel safe. In turn, they learned it from *their* parents, and so on. This pattern of behavior was established in our childhood by suppressing our own feelings (wishes and desires) so that we could obey the rules established by family/society - what is good/ bad, right/wrong, what we should/shouldn't do.

For every "good" and "right" we gained approval and it meant survival. We applied this parental behavior pattern later to the world. In the majority of cases, if we want to be loved by someone, we are trying to "please" him/her and suppress all our own feelings in order to get approval for our actions and words. We do the same things in our marriages, picking at each other most of the time, looking for ego approval. Desire for approval is the strongest motivating force for us and an "indicator"/feedback mechanism about how much we are loved.

In truth, what most of us call love is in fact *need,* and it is conditional, manipulative, and exclusive. How often are we looking for appreciation from our mate, relatives, employer, colleagues, and friends, in order to feel that we are "good" and loved?

We substitute approval for love, looking for it in others, struggling hard for it and spending all our effort in a desire to get it. We rely and depend on others' opinions, and if others disapprove of us, we feel frustrated, depressed, and don't want to accept ourselves the way we are. Our self-esteem goes down and we begin suffering from not being loved. We are blind to the fact that the love we are looking for lies within us and is part of our infinite state of being.

But if love is an inherent part of our being and is inside us, how come we don't know about it and can't feel it?

- First, we lost the connection with our selves (infinite being=soul=Love=God) a long time ago and now our logical mind can't accept it and let us believe in it without logical/ scientific explanation.
- Secondly, we are always looking away from it (looking for love/ happiness in other people, things, events), rather than looking toward it (the need to dive "within" until we see the reality of who we are).
- Thirdly, although many people say that they love themselves, in fact they have no idea of the true meaning of love, and even if they become aware of it, they don't know how to "dive" within, express and maintain this state of love.

The paradox is that love is our inherent state and is within us. We either have it or we don't: it can't be turned on and off.

What does this mean?

It means that we can have love (experience a state of joy and happiness) to the degree we perceive this world through the prism of love and accept it the way it is. If you want to know how much self-love you have inside you, check your thoughts, look at the world around you and see how much love is there.

A strong indicator for love is your attitude toward others: if you can love and accept people the way they are and feel love even toward those who hate you. To receive love and be loved, we *must* have the feeling of love inside us, because what we give out must come back. We often substitute self-appreciation for self-love, doing something pleasant for our self (buying a gift, going on vacation etc.) and thinking that this is true self-love, but it isn't. Often when we make gifts for others, we are looking for something in return, and if they don't give it to us, we blame them for not loving us.

Let's imagine for a second that you have a beautiful "vessel" inside your chest, full of sparking energy that comes from the universal source. This sparking energy is your soul, your infinite being, your self-love that you are looking for.

In general we're not aware of what an infinite being is, and how powerful it is. This "vessel" is covered by many layers of disbelief, dogmas, and illusions, all of which we've been exposed to since birth, so much so that we can't see or feel any of it clearly.

In addition, our logical mind with its noisy thoughts is sitting on the top of the vessel and clouding our connection with the Source. But unconsciously we continue to seek our infinite self all the time, calling it love and happiness. We are trying to escape from worries and fearful thoughts (which are painful) by going on vacation, partying, socializing, and dating in order to feel happy and secure. These things give us some brief relief, but take us away from the source of joy that is within us.

We try to achieve "important" goals, positions, and titles; they make us feel real, they feed our egos and help us feel happier, but at some point we must realize that deep inside in our soul we feel lonely. In desperation we are knocking at the closed door of our mate, crying and begging for love but get only silence in return ... *Why?*

Do you know how many layers of disbelief and dogmas are covering *your* vessel? If the Source of Love is within you, but you don't belief in yourself, or are not aware of who you are, how then can you love yourself? If you don't have self-love, then how can you love others? How can others give it to you if they don't have it?

Looking for love without loving doesn't bring love to you, doesn't satisfy you. You can't give away what you don't have. The feeling of love has to be *in* you. Love is a state of self: it is something you *are*.

To find love (yourself) you need to dive within, dig within, have a real understanding of universal laws, and of who you are. When you discover who you are, you will be able to accept yourself the *way* you are—and this is the first step toward self-love, it's when you discover why you came into the world and find answers to all your questions.

When you know who you are and see the reality of yourself, you'll know that you—your true self—are perfect and omnipresent (as gurus and masters teach us). When you find your true self, then you will find God, love and peace.

It is your journey ... of letting go of your thoughts of limitations and the transformation of your belief system, which in turn changes your perception of the world, your consciousness. You will love the world the way it is rather than trying to change it and you will accept and love others the way they are: fully, wholly, and totally.

This attitude of love is the key to your healing! When you're able to understand the true meaning of love and what it means to love yourself, when you're able to express and maintain this state, *then* you will be able to unlock your inner power and true miracles will begin to happen in your life. To love yourself means to *become* love (experience a state of joy and happiness) by increasing your level of consciousness (vibrational frequencies of our thoughts and feelings) toward the world, to see its perfection, and accept it the way it is.

In December 2012, planet earth, along with humanity, entered the fifth dimension, which is a dimension of love - true unconditional love. The "end of the world" meant a transition in humanity's general consciousness from the third dimension of low-frequency vibrations - the world of the logical left brain which had an effect on our thinking, feeling, and acting; the concept of unconditional love couldn't exist there - to the fifth dimension—a higher frequency of vibrations which bring possibilities to return to our inherent state of love and reach radiant health and abundance.

To move into the fifth dimension we must release all our mental and emotional baggage from the third dimension (which means letting go of emotional trauma, negative thoughts and feelings) and become masters of our mind. We are all moving in this direction now, and you can't escape it. So if life challenging you, it is your time to drop the old baggage of painful memories and emotions and become love. Just stay with your open heart and learn how to love yourself.

Let's step into this journey and assume that what the gurus and masters tell us is true, that our infinite being (our true self) is always perfect and omnipresent. If that's true, could I have this knowledge that I was healthy - when diagnosed with cancer - through deep connection with myself, my infinite being?

This knowledge was extraordinarily strong inside me. When I was trying to convince others of it, however, nobody could believe, and I felt as if there was a brick wall between us and I couldn't break through it. Later on, when my cancer was gone, Irina admitted that she would probably not have believed my story had she not witnessed it herself.

From my experience I learned that all answers to the questions I was asking were hidden behind the understanding of the logical mind, and if I wanted to succeed in my journey, I needed to keep an open mind and accept information/knowledge—even if it seemed illogical and if science couldn't yet fully explain it.

Now, when I became aware of what love is, I needed to rediscover how this self-realization could help me heal and stay healthy.

At that point I was wondering why must we have sick bodies, why is there suffering and dying from cancer and other diseases if we (our self) are perfect and infinite. *If perfection of our self is real and the world we live is an illusion (which is what the most enlightened spiritual teachers teach) does it mean that a sick body is an illusion too? Then, if a sick body is an illusion, can we reverse it to perfection—or at least help it to heal?*

CHAPTER FOURTEEN:

What Physics Tells Us

"All matter originates and exists only by virtue of a force, which brings the particle of an atom to vibration and holds this most minute solar system of the atom together. We must assume behind this force the existence of a conscious and intelligent mind. This mind is a matrix of all matter."
—Max Planck (Nobel Prize winner, physicist who developed quantum theory)

B efore we dive within, let's dig into what physics tells us about the universe.

In the 17th century, based on Isaac Newton's theory, it was believed that the universe was made of small solid particles called atoms, attracted to each other by gravity.

Then, in the 19th century, Albert Einstein proved that atoms are *not* solid particles and that they can be divided further into smaller subatomic particles, which at their core consist of pure energy. These subatomic particles have a very high rate of vibration that creates what we can think of as a vision of a solid object.

This discovery meant that everything in the universe (earth, nature, people, cars, thoughts, emotions … everything) when broken down to its most basic form (molecules, atoms, subatomic particles, energy) consists of a vibrating mass of pure energy of different frequencies.

Einstein thought that this energy had a form of particles, in opposition to another physicist, Tomas Young, who believed that energy can exist in the form of wave. Nobel Prize-winner Niels Bohr was convinced that energy could present in both forms: waves and particles. The most accepted explanation for wave-particle duality (why the same subatomic particle may behave in different ways, e.g., as waves and particles) was given in what's called the *Copenhagen interpretation*, in which quantum physics made the first general attempt to understand the world of atoms.

The Copenhagen interpretation reveals that a quantum of (subatomic) particles doesn't exist in one state or another, but in all possible states at once, and could manifest itself either as a wave or a particle, depending on the circumstances. Subatomic particles are forced to choose either particle or wave form based on the individual thoughts of the scientist studying the phenomenon.

In other words, it's only when a scientist observes energy (when an observer pays attention to it) that energy transmutes and appears either as a particle or wave—based on the observer's belief, thoughts, and expectations. Later on, when these subatomic particles were separated in laboratory settings, it was discovered that they could remain in communication through vibration regardless of the distance, and attract other particles/energies that had the same frequency.

So if everything in the universe is energy, which has that ability to communicate without regard to space and time, and change its shape based on thoughts, then our thoughts are very powerful weapons indeed.

Our minds and bodies operate according to a universal law of cause-and-effect, which states that every single thought can materialize in the physical world. So everything that happens *to* us, is created *by* us! If you keep an open mind and can accept this truth, you will come to the realization that *you are responsible for everything that has happened to you and the world around you is a projection of your inner state.*

Let's see how this works at the body-mind-spirit level. Are you ready to dive within?

CHAPTER FIFTEEN:

What is Soul?

*"He who created us without our help will not
save us without our consent."*
—Saint Augustine

O nce upon a time, there was a soul (spirit) who lost her identity
while being in a physical body, and was unconsciously
looking for self, calling it love. The mind, with its self-limiting
perception, was trying to give a logical definition of love and earn that
love through approval - but was moving in the opposite direction. There
was a conflict, since the mind could offer only an *illusion* of love, but the
soul was looking for the real thing.

This continued until one day the body was diagnosed with an
incurable disease. This situation forced the mind to turn toward the soul,
surrender to God and ask her soul for guidance.

We are multi-dimensional beings. As a soul (Spirit=Infinite being=
Love=Self=Energy=Light) we are connected with the infinite source

(Universal Consciousness/Intelligence=Higher Power=God) and all universal laws apply to us. We come to planet earth for the development of our souls—and it is a school for all of us.

The soul is infinite, perfect and omnipresent. There are young souls, which are in the first grade and there are those that are in tenth grade. Every soul has to go through its own unique life, or program, based on previous life experience, facing and overcoming challenges—just as if it were passing an exam to go from one grade to another.

In order to exist on this planet, the soul needs a physical body, and in order to function, it needs a mind. According to quantum physicists, the entire universe is nothing but a ball of vibrating energy that can communicate and carry information into infinity with no regard to space or time. Our physical body is a vibrating mass of atoms and it links to our energy-body through the chakras. Chakras are the concentrated energy centers through which the physical body is constantly receiving, assimilating, and transmitting life-force energy drawn from the universe through the crown chakra.

All chakras are interrelated and interdependent. They have seven colors and resonate at seven vibrational frequencies. The first root chakra has the lowest frequency and the seventh crown chakra has the highest.

The energy field we're part of and exposed to from birth (our family and society with its belief system, dogmas, attitudes, rules) is encoded, generated, and processed as information in our chakras. After this information is processed, it is integrated around our own field of energy and forms our thoughts, emotions, beliefs, feelings, attitudes and … well, our life!

Basically, our chakras represent information on our world perception by dividing it into different spheres - first chakra: family, work, finances; second chakra: sex, creativity, etc.

It's important that energy can flow freely with no blockages. If we have unreleased emotions from past experience, such as fear, anger, jealousy or lack of nurturing and love, we'll create energy blocks that affect our mental and physical health.

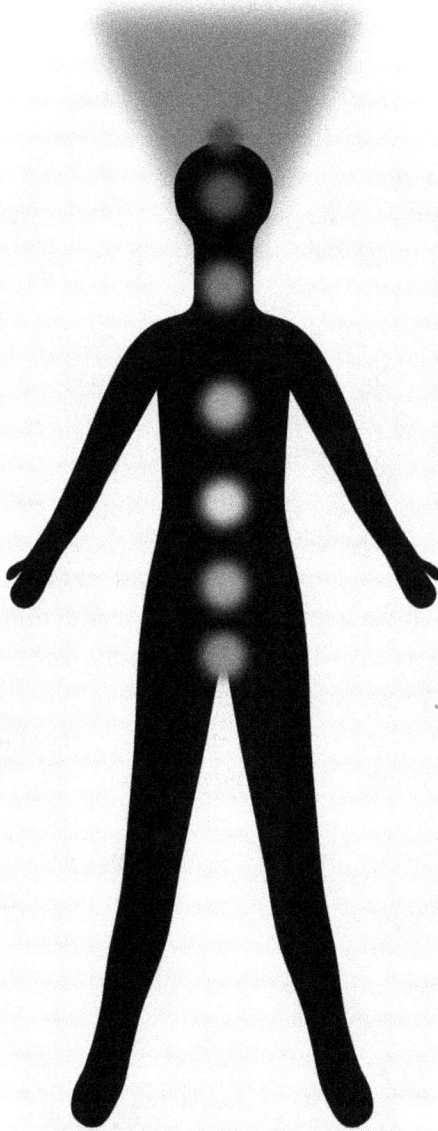

If we have a negative attitude toward something or somebody, or strongly object to it/them, then the vibrational frequencies (energy) of our thoughts and feelings will project into our own energy field and attract the same vibrations in the universe, transmuting from waves into particles of matter. Do you remember how subatomic particles behaved during the laboratory experiment when they were separated? They attracted other particles/energies with the same frequency.

So if you vibrate at a low frequency with negativity, you will attract the same low frequency energy—one that forms and brings negative events into your life. This will keep happening until you change your attitude toward this subject/object and learn to accept it the way it is.

We are all in a school called life and came here to learn and grow. So our chakras dictate our world perception: it's a foundation we stand upon, which contains instruction on how to behave in the world, based on programmed beliefs and attitudes.

Our life experiences depend on the information encoded in this foundation. This will determine the range of vibrational life frequencies used by each one of us. The vibrational frequencies determine our individual ways of perceiving and understanding surrounding realities.

We look at the world through our own prism, which has a different angle of view depending on the grade we are.

So how is this information related to cancer patients?

It is your physical body (a 'suitcase') that has a cancer and it is an illusion. You are neither a physical body nor a mind. The truth is that you are a perfect and infinite being. The degree to which you accept this is the degree to which you will heal.

1. You have inside yourself the natural power and ability to heal from cancer; you just need to listen your heart and follow your soul. Instead, by forgetting this you are limiting yourself.
2. In order to heal, you need to dive within and bring back all your energy and restore its flow by letting go of all emotional pain and forgiving yourself and others. This return of emotional energy

will allow previously clogged energies of life to fully circulate, nourish and detoxify your entire being. You need to find your true self, your identity. You need to let go of concepts of lack and limitation, go within, and see this unlimited being. This consciousness shift will trigger a transformational process in you and allow the body to restore itself to full health.

3. If you can remove blockages and restore energy flow by forgiveness and letting go of emotional pain, but remain surrounded by your old environment and negative energies (family members, work situation, which trigger negative feelings in you), and you don't change your perception toward it (attitude, world outlook) you can create the same blockages again and cause a recurrence of disease. Complete resolution of the cancer on the MRI doesn't mean complete cure—and cancer can come back at any time if you remain surrounded by an environment that triggers negative feelings in you and you continue to send your energy toward it. For patients who are currently in remission or those who were able to melt cancer away from their body, but still have concerns about the possibility of it coming back, this book can give guidance on how to achieve full recovery. Complete healing requires not only restoring energy flow by unplugging from the past through forgiveness and letting go of painful memories and emotional trauma, but also the ability to keep these energies in the present by withdrawing from such situations and changing your perception toward them. *It is all about you!* It is a journey of inner transformation, and when you start from yourself, the whole world around you will change. This is why many people who overcome cancer have to make drastic changes in their life; they undergo a transformative process by upgrading their attitudes and belief system. The degree of change you have to make in your life will depend on your particular situation. This does not mean that everyone has to go through these drastic changes. But in general, if you are changing, expect—and accept—changes around you.

4. When you discover the real you, you will discover true love. When you come to the realization of what love is and can maintain that attitude, you'll stay healthy and free from cancer forever.

CHAPTER SIXTEEN:

What is Mind?

"Mind is consciousness, which has put on limitations. You are originally unlimited and perfect. Later you take on limitations and become a mind."
—Ramana Maharshi.

Y ou will take what I have to say here as truth, or you will take it as a tale, and how you take it is based on your perception of the world (your level of consciousness).

When my mind surrendered to God, the soul reveals the truth.

It was a shock for the mind. The mind was rebelling and didn't want to admit this truth. The ego was supporting the mind and stated that there is only one "I" (ego), separated from others and didn't want to admit to being subordinate to the soul. The mind was threatened and felt it could be wiped out if the ego were to be destroyed, so the mind was trying to protect itself by making the body busy. The soul was watching silently from above and knew that the noisy mind and ego couldn't see her until they went quiet …

The mind is an instrument for our soul to function in the physical body and create our world. It is a composite of our thoughts (conscious and subconscious) and feelings.

The mind and body operate by the universal law of cause-and-effect. What am I talking about? Quantum physics tells us that everything in the universe is a ball of vibrating intelligent energy (information) so our thoughts and emotions are part of it and obey its laws.

MIND

CONSCIOUS THOUGHTS
FEELINGS (EMOTIONS)

SUBCONSCIOUS THOUGHTS
FEELINGS (EMOTIONS)

Let's look at how it works.

If we look at the mind, we see that it consists of conscious and unconscious thoughts and feelings. The conscious thoughts are those we think and are aware of in the present moment and occupy a small part of the mind. The conscious mind is dominant, and its main role is to analyze, filter, and process data. The conscious mind makes resolutions regarding received information and labels that information as right/wrong, true/false, based on the established belief system, then attaches emotion to the thought and sends it to the subconscious mind. Later on, this information can be accessed to support or discredit future data received by the conscious mind.

However, the major part of the mind belongs to the *subconscious*, which holds hundreds of thousands of thoughts we're usually unaware of in the present moment. The primary function of the subconscious mind is to record and store data (like a hard drive in a computer) received from the conscious mind.

When processed information downloads into the subconscious mind, it remains active all the time. What does that mean? It means that even though our thoughts and feelings are unconscious, they are *active*.

How does this work? It works through the autonomic nervous system by managing and controlling subconscious bodily functioning (heart rate, breathing, cellular function) and broadcasting the vibrational frequency of the stored data to the universe 24/7. As a result, those vibrational frequencies (the energy) of the stored data attract the same vibrational energy intensity from the universe and form our reality in the physical world.

What we give out, we get back.

The world around us is a projection of what is in our mind. We have buried and hidden all the painful and negative thoughts and feelings from the past in our subconscious mind, and now they're actively running us. If we broadcast our pain and negativity to the universe, we will get it back—not realizing why we're facing this situation again and again and attracting it into our life! We go on and on behaving automatically and become victims of our subconscious minds.

If you surround yourself with negative information (anything negative you see, hear, or sense) this information downloads into your subconscious mind and runs your life automatically by attracting similar situations. If you're silently present during your friend/employer's angry outburst and suppress your emotions, you absorb and download this anger to your subconscious mind. If you fight it, it means you resist it—and then it grows. Then you are in a vicious cycle.

Now look around and see what's surrounding you. Are you aware that you have been running your life unconsciously, thinking that you're a victim of random circumstances … but in fact you are not? When you understand the universal law of cause-and-effect and know how your mind and body operate based on it, you become a conscious creator of your new reality.

So the universal law of cause-and-effect states that for every cause (action, thought, word, or feeling) there must be an equal effect (outcome). What we send out to the universe, we get back. *This is the language with which we communicate with the universe.* The universal law of cause-and-effect correlates with the quantum physics principle that everything in the world, when broken down to its basic form, consists of energy or vibration and attracts vibrational frequencies of the same intensity by manifesting in the physical world as reality.

So as thought is an energy or vibration, it has the power to form events and circumstances in your life that match the frequency of your thoughts. If your thoughts carry the energy of lower vibrational frequency (fear, anger and jealousy, for example) they will join with the same vibrational frequencies in the universe and manifest or create similar events and situations that you'll then have to face in order to experience this feeling again.

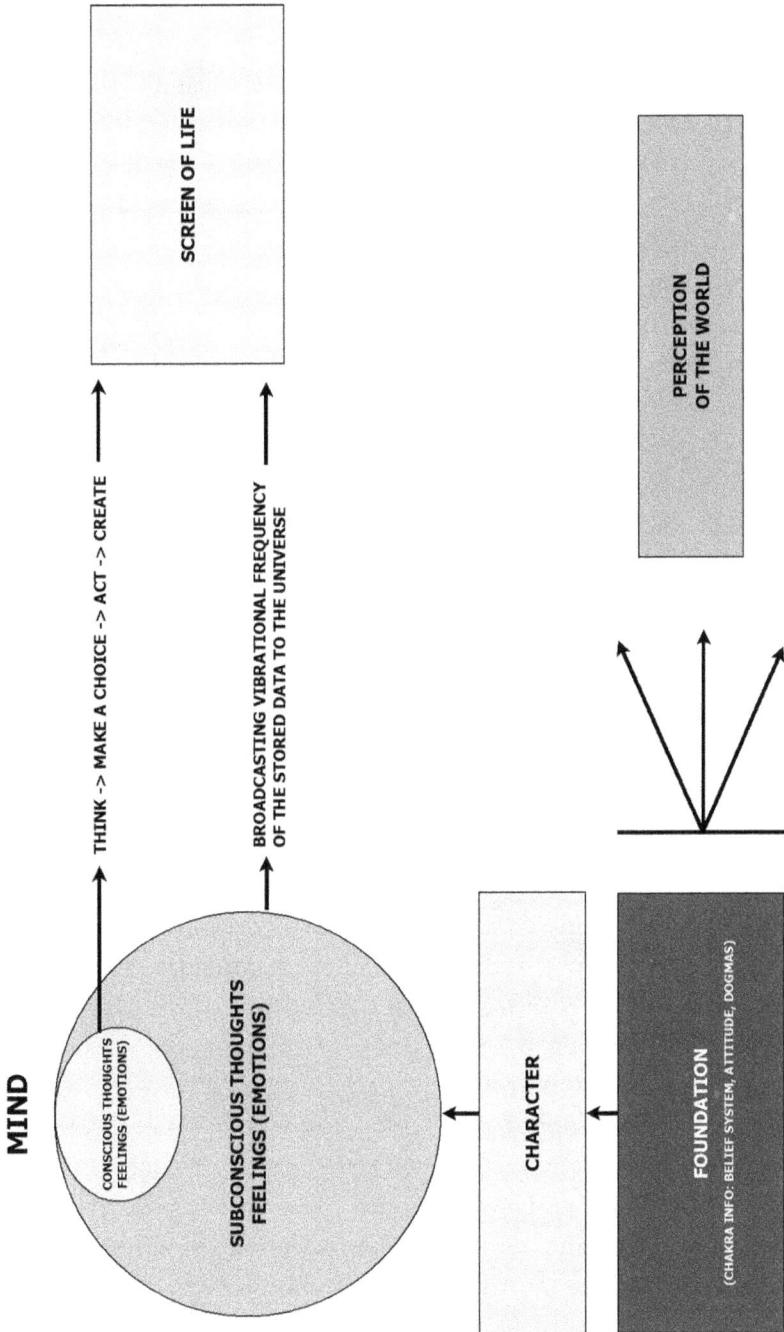

This continues until one day you can accept what is happening and begin *your* journey of growth and understanding of the truth.

If you know the truth, you know that God is all, and God is perfect.

As a perfect infinite being (soul) you came to this planet for your soul's further development. Before you descended here, you were conditioned for certain experiences and learning opportunities you would need to go through to realize your goal.

This is why you born into a certain family and society with its beliefs, rules, and attitudes, or why you were perhaps exposed to traumatic childhood situations. The energy field you were part of and surrounded by was downloaded, encoded, generated and processed as information in your chakras to meet the preset goal.

This information informed your beliefs, rules and attitude and formed the foundation that has built your character, determined your perception of the world and ruled your life. So every challenging situation we face in our lives was something that we actually attracted and was given to us as a lesson to help us learn and grow.

We are broadcasting to the universe on the vibrational frequency of our thoughts (coupled with feelings) and the universe mirrors our inner state by creating events and circumstances in our outer world.

Learning your lesson through true forgiveness, understanding and acceptance means changing your foundation - attitudes, beliefs and dogmas. In turn, changing your foundation will change your character and perception of the world (your level of consciousness). The prism through which you look at the world will have a broader view.

And just as you see different prisms of light and color when you look through a kaleidoscope, soon you will see a different, more beautiful and changing picture of the world in its perfection!

We are the creators of our world; we create it with our mind, our thoughts and our feelings. To become the master of your mind means to live in the present and be consciously aware of what you are creating.

Our mind operates only within the spectrum of visible light and can't perceive and see information that is outside it. So it's very difficult to acknowledge information not within the spectrum of the logical mind-vision and agree with it. It's difficult to acknowledge that our thoughts and feelings are energy and they can run our lives and create our reality.

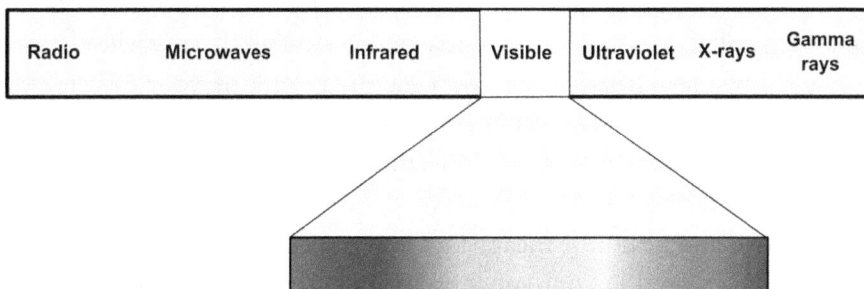

Radio	Microwaves	Infrared	Visible	Ultraviolet	X-rays	Gamma rays

But here's the good news: you don't have to understand how it works! All you have to do is keep an open heart and mind, and give yourself a chance to win over cancer by believing in this possibility.

How is this information related to cancer patients?

Based on the universal law of cause-and-effect, a problem exists as long as you consciously think about it. When you try to get *rid* of the problem, what you are really doing is resisting it—and, therefore, holding onto it.

It's vitally important that cancer patients accept their cancer with love and gratitude, that they see it as a means of transformation into the "new you." If you fight the cancer, you will let it grow: it's a crisis of your soul! Your soul is crying and telling you that it is too tight to be in a physical body, to see the world through your limited-view prism, and live the life you live. It's a message for you that your foundation, with its old beliefs and attitudes toward the world, is not working anymore. You need to change this foundation if you want your soul to develop further, and changing the foundation will change your world-perception and make your view of the world far bigger than ever before.

This is your wake-up call! Be grateful to the universe for this opportunity and the universe will unfold its mystery for you.

It's very important to be grateful for both bad and good things that happen in our lives. There is a deep meaning behind it all. You're embarked on a journey within, to know who you are and what the world and the universe are. Such a journey requires strong belief and strong desire, both of which will help you develop a new understanding of yourself.

You must also learn how to become the master of your own mind. This means that you need to know how to become consciously aware of the piles of rubbish you are constantly downloading there. It means that you need to learn to consciously control it and program yourself toward love and health. It means that you can change and overwrite the existing data stored in your subconscious mind and attract harmonized frequency vibrations.

When you do that, anything that your mind is totally convinced of materializes in the physical world. Every harmful thought, word, or action creates a dark energy blockage in your own system, drops the level of your vibration, and decreases love energy.

You create your own reality. So you should believe that you are healthy— feel and see yourself as healthy right now. If you can maintain an attitude of love, which has the *highest* vibration, the cancer will melt away and never come back. Think about your thoughts and emotions and what you are doing with your life.

Remember that your noisy mind is the only thing that's keeping you from the realization of your infinite self. You need to learn how to quieten your mind in order to express your higher self.

The truth is that our feelings and our thinking are what create everything that happens to us. *The world around you is a projection of what is in your mind. So it's very important to let go of all your negative thoughts and emotions, to forgive, and to focus on the positive.*

The power of gratitude and forgiveness clears the energy blockages in your system. Since our minds have been automatically running us for millions of years, it is not easy to reprogram, especially when facing an incurable disease - but it can be done, you just need to believe in it! Until you make the internal changes necessary, your external result will stay exactly the same.

Keep looking within. Many people try to change their partners, and that's simply wrong. Never blame others. Your partner is looking at this world through his or her own prism downloaded in childhood and have their own perspective and worldview— God has given that to them for specific reasons, too. What you are trying to do is to criticize and blame their God program and replace it with your own: but everyone has their own path, their own journey to make.

Can you see what you're doing and why you've been facing the same situation again and again? Start changing yourself and the world around you will change! It is you who created and attracted the situation you're in and you need it for the growth and development of your soul. It's the vibrational frequencies of your data, downloaded to your chakras during your childhood, that's broadcasting to the universe through your subconscious mind and attracting situations and people of the same vibration that you need to help you face your challenges and learn your lesson.

When you know the truth, you'll be able to understand that if there's anything that annoys you in other people, it's only because you have it in you. If you didn't have it in you, you couldn't even see it in others!

You also need to learn to be consciously aware of what and whom you surround yourself with. What people and situations do you expose yourself to, and what information (data) are you actively absorbing into your subconscious mind? It is crucial for you to be surrounded by love and care. You need it until you're able to gain some inner strength and understanding and generate love by yourself.

Stop blaming others for your disease, and stop feeling sorry for yourself. Instead, you should program your mind to know that you are a perfect being, and healthy.

You need to be honest with yourself, trust yourself, follow your heart, and have enough inner power to let go of old relationships that are not fulfilling. Maybe you will need to change your job or physical location - this is the hardest part of the journey, which many people are not ready to do. When there is a cancer patient in a family, it is always a journey for two people (you and your partner). It will either bring your

97

relationship to a much higher level of understanding and love, or it will destroy the relationship, but either way it can never be the same again.

Otherwise, the universe will be challenging you again and again (since your vibrational frequency will not change) with even harder trials, until you cannot stand it anymore. If you don't know what to do, *listen to your heart*. Your heart will guide you. You need to understand that you can't build a new life, a new you, and go through the necessary transformation (which you need in order for your soul to go through the crisis and completely heal) based on the old foundation. To build a new belief system and attitude toward the world, you need to adjust and reconsider or let go of the old one. This is the purpose of this journey.

It is your cure!

CHAPTER SEVENTEEN:

What is the Physical Body?

*"What is a physical body? "The greatest mistake
physicians make is that they attempt to cure
the body without attempting to cure the mind;
yet the mind and the body are one and should
not be treated separately."*
—Plato

As I said before, you will take what I'm about to say as truth, or
you will take it as a tale based on your own world-perception -
your level of consciousness.

The mind knows that the body operates according to the law of
cause-and-effect, and will do whatever the mind thinks. Since the body is
seemingly material and real, nobody guesses that it's only a holographic
illusion, an exact copy of the mind. The mind wants to keep this

conspiracy alive, since it gives the mind a chance to overshadow the soul and take priority over it.

For thousands of years, the soul in its perfection was hidden from the general view for sacred reasons, and all attempts to treat the physical body (which is a suitcase or shell through which our higher self operates and experiences reality on earth) with incurable disease ended in a fiasco. This state of affairs continued until December 21, 2012, a date originally thought to herald the end of the world, but in fact signaling a transformational shift in general consciousness. It was a shift from the third dimension to the fifth dimension, which is the dimension of love.

To make it happen, to go through this shift, many people found themselves facing a crisis in various areas of their lives (health, personal, social, financial) until they reached the point when they attributed it all to God. The mind couldn't keep up the conspiracy anymore and the soul revealed the truth. The old foundation was ruined and replaced by a new one, which broadened the prism's spectrum and changed the world's perception, its level of consciousness. The old human consciousness system was destroyed and a new one took its place. People started awakening to their infinity and true power to heal and become love.

It might not sound realistic, but the truth is that our bodies follow the universal law of cause-and-effect, and we're talking about an effect of the mind. *It means that your body is only an outward projection of what is in your mind and you can change your body mentally - you can heal or reshape it.*

Probably here your logical mind is beginning to protest and think, "If it's so easy to achieve the desired result, then it doesn't make sense that we struggle so hard to cure incurable diseases, to lose weight, to be in a good shape ... if it's so easy, then everybody should have a perfect healthy body!"

Well, there are good reasons why it doesn't happen that way.

Firstly, can you really believe, can you be convinced 100 percent, that you are a perfect infinite being, that your physical body is a creation of your mind, and a sick or fat body is an illusion? Of course not! You've been trapped, programmed by your logical mind, which wants to keep you under its authority for another thousand years. But be mindful of this: *the degree to which you can accept and believe in it is the degree to which you will heal.*

Secondly, let's look at what we are doing. Cancer patients' minds are full of thoughts and fear of death and they are fighting cancer. Those who want to lose weight do everything to overcome their problem with diets and exercise but rarely achieve the desired results. Why? Because our body is outward projection of your mind, and the thoughts you hold there (fear, fighting, problems) will attract the same energies in the universe and you will have what you have. It's only when you truly desire to become the master of your mind and consciously control your thoughts that you will be able to change.

Thirdly, in order to have or become what you want, it's not enough to just wipe out negative thoughts from your conscious mind, you have to replace them with something else. You must reload your subconscious mind with a new program. You're never going to have the desired result until you are convinced of it subconsciously as well as consciously - and that's a very difficult thing to do!

When you know who you are, and what the world is, you discover the reality of the body and the world. You discover the reality that you are a perfect infinite being and that your sick body is an illusion.

To understand this requires a high level of self-awareness, something we all need to be moving toward. In the past only gurus, masters, or saints—or those who had a near-death experience—could have this realization, but after 2012 (when this transformation process began with a shift in general consciousness) more and more people are waking up to see their own perfection.

How does this information relate to cancer patients?

- You can heal yourself. You have the power inside to do it. You are the one who has to launch your healing program.
- Your success depends on your own belief in a positive outcome, your acceptance of your own perfection, coupled with an inner desire and determination complete this journey.

- In order to cure cancer, you have to awaken from the illusion you've been in, realize who you are, accept the unity of body, mind, and spirit, and acknowledge your connection with the universal source.

Cancer can be cured when the true nature of body-mind-spirit unity is recognized, understood, and accepted. It means acceptance of our true identity in the context of body-mind-spirit unity and our connection with the universal source. It means an acknowledgment of the natural energy of the universe and its laws.

We haven't been able to find a cure for a cancer for many thousands of years because we lost our true identity. We no longer knew who we were; our target for treatment was the physical body - which we are not! The truth is that we are multidimensional beings, an infinite being or soul in a physical body functioning through a mind in different dimensions: planet earth for our physical body and mind, and universe for our soul.

The reality is that you can heal your body using different levels of the body-mind-spirit approach:

1. **The spiritual level:** The highest and quickest way of healing is on the spiritual level, through complete surrender to God, using spiritual practices such as prayers, meditation, self-realization, forgiveness, spiritual remedies and energy transmission. Whether or not you can do it depends on your level of personal self- awareness.

2. **The mental level:** Healing at this level can take longer—from weeks to months, depending on your mental concept—than healing on the spiritual level, but everyone can do it. You need to become master of your mind by dropping all negative thoughts and quieting your mind. You need to learn how to consciously control your thoughts and move them toward your goal, letting go of your emotions, and forgiving.

3. **The physical level:** Think of your body as a suitcase. You're not going to cure an incurable disease by just working on the suitcase, even if that is the standard protocol. You have to pay attention to what's *inside* the suitcase! You're facing a crisis of

your soul: it's a time for growth, for upgrading your system, within and without.

Even if a sick body is an illusion, it doesn't mean that you don't need to do anything at the physical level. It's very important to clean, detoxify, nurture and energize your body. So what about the standard protocol? If you believe in it, follow it. But your treatment shouldn't be directed *only* towards the physical body: to achieve full recovery you will need to approach cancer from the body-mind-spirit vision. If you don't believe in it, don't follow it. You need to make a choice based on your belief, foundation system, your readiness to overcome your disease, and your faith in creating your reality and your own outcome. Whatever choice you make, this choice will be right and perfect for you. But be sure to approach it from a calm comfort zone. Don't rub yourself in the fear; believe in your recovery; know and always remember that you are an infinite perfect being; and see yourself being already healed—open your heart and keep an attitude of love!

Remember that the power of healing is inside you, and that it is *you* who will heal yourself, not somebody else. Whatever you are doing, it is important for your recovery to follow the recommendations provided for the spiritual and mental levels.

CHAPTER EIGHTEEN:

The Spiritual Level of Body, Mind, and Spirit

"O Holy Spirit, descend plentifully into my heart.
Enlighten the dark corners of this neglected
dwelling and scatter there Thy cheerful beams."
—Saint Augustine

L et's take a look at what you can actually do at this level, and at how it might be done. We'll start with the spiritual level.

SPIRIT: You can find the lost connection with your soul - inherent love - through:

1. **Prayer:** Prayer helps you obtain a deeper state of consciousness and allows you to receive Divine Grace. But first you need to relearn how to pray. True prayer isn't asking for something. It isn't the "petition prayer" you've gotten used to: "O God, why

me? O God, can you give me this, and in return I promise to ..." You need to know how to experience prayer at the deepest and most profound level. You need to surrender to God! A super source that I recommend highly is a video web-stream called *The Power of Meditation and Prayer* by Caroline Myss.[9]

2. **Meditation:** What does meditation do and why is it so important? First of all, it helps *quieten your mind* and frees you of the loud and noisy thoughts that live there and keep you away from infinite being. Only when your mind is quiet will you become receptive and connected to your higher self and that's when you can come to self-realization about who you are—and what the world is. Meditation triggers your spiritual awakening and brings your yin and yang energy into balance. Meditation enables this higher energy to remove your energy blocks and heal you instantly. In meditation, you can ask questions. In meditation, you can find peace.

3. **Energy transmission:** I have personally experienced energy transmission and believe in it. But that doesn't mean that if you receive it, you will automatically be healed! What I believe is that energy transmission can help you to initiate the process of healing in yourself, but the outcome will completely depend on your readiness, desire, and participation. It is your soul going through the crisis, and it is you who has the power to heal yourself—and nobody but you. You need to search inside and find the power to go through this transformative process. This is the purpose of your journey, and in order to be completely cured it should be "fixed" by you. When you dive within, you'll clear blockages (letting go of emotional pain, anger and fear) and then divine energies will induce your healing. Start with yourself, accept your own power, stay open and believe in energy transmission, but don't be blindly dependent on others - and don't expect healing to be done for you. If you don't have the ability to heal, nobody

---

[9] (http://store.myss.com/the-power-of-meditation-and-prayer-p1810.aspx

will be able to help you. Some of the people who may be helpful to you on your journey are Adam McLeod,[10] Panache Desai,[11] and Mahendra Kumar Trivedi.[12]

---

[10] (http://www.dreamhealer.com/)

[11] (http://www.panachedesai.com)

[12] (http://trivedimasterwellness.com/about/trivedi-bio/)

CHAPTER NINETEEN:

The Mental Level of Body, Mind and Spirit

"One of the greatest discoveries is that a human being can alter his life by altering his attitudes of mind."
—William James

Believe it or not, you are actually in control of your mental level. You are perfectly capable of quieting your noisy mind and taking control of the thoughts you don't want to be there. Negative thoughts attract negative energy, because it's what they're putting out. Positive thoughts attract positive energy, because it's what they put out.

Here are some suggestions to help you regain your quietness and peace:

- Positive affirmations (in particular Louise L. Hay's affirmation system)

- Mantras - they work as repeated affirmations that lead to concentration of thought.
- Chanting - can work in the same way as mantras.
- Becoming consciously aware of your thoughts. When a negative thought enters your mind, drop it and bring in a positive thought. Over time this will become easier, until only the thoughts you want will enter your mind.
- Sing a song that makes you happy.
- Laugh.
- Visualization of your desired outcome should associate with positive feelings. I cannot stress enough how vital this is.
- Use breathing techniques to clean negative thoughts from your body at the cellular level.

In addition to these exercises and techniques, there's something else you have to do, something that is crucial to your recovery, and that is forgiving and letting go of emotional pain. Here too there are some techniques:

- Releasing - emotional freedom techniques, Larry Crane's releasing techniques, going into a space where no one can hear you and screaming, or beating a punch ball or pillow.
- Healing unhealthy attitudes and toxic decisions.

CHAPTER TWENTY:

The Physical Level of the Body, Mind, and Spirit

"Begin to see yourself as a soul with a body rather than a body with a soul."
—Wayne W. Dyer

W hen a cancer patient faces this diagnosis they need a lot of support from their partner and family members. I would also say that usually caregivers are in need of this support, too.

What is happening is that a cancer patient's "downloaded" foundation system of beliefs, attitudes, and old rules must be shut down and replaced with a new, healthy foundation.

People surrounding the patient are accustomed to the old system just as much as the patient is and they often subconsciously become threatened by the fact that the new upgraded system (changes) will affect their own well-being. There is often resistance from those close to the patient, and that must be taken into account.

It's therefore essential for you, the patient, to remain true to yourself even if you don't have their support at first. Make your decisions based on what you agreed upon with yourself and what resources (human, financial) are available to you.

The spiritual and mental approaches described here depend completely on your desire to do them; but at the physical level your approach will depend on the decision you made and resources you have.

So the recommendations written below will need to be adjusted for the direction in which you are moving. *For those navigating the chemo-surgery-radiation protocol, talk to your doctor and ask which of these is appropriate for you.* It is important to realize that no matter which direction you're navigating, either traditional or non-traditional, you need to be comfortable and at peace with your decision and believe in your recovery. For those who choose the alternative pathway, detoxing via your diet must be on the list.

Vegan diet: there are a variety of diet systems available today for cancer patients. But if you compare them, you may find contradictions. It happens, don't go crazy! Choose just one with which you feel comfortable (ask your heart) and stick with it. What I learned was that it's important to keep your blood pH level alkaline, which any vegan diet will do for you. If you do choose the vegan route, here's some food that will be helpful:

- asparagus
- almonds
- beets
- berries (blueberries, blackberries, strawberries, raspberries)
- broccoli
- cabbage
- carrots
- cauliflower
- chlorella
- citrus fruit juices (oranges, lemon and limes)

- green tea
- garlic
- grapes
- lentils (beans and peas, too!)
- oats
- omega3 oils (flaxseed oil and cottage cheese in the Budwig Diet)
- onions
- tomatoes
- peppers
- apples

Body Detoxification: This is super-important. Personally I found Dr. Richard Schulze's to be one of the best,[13] but you can choose any one you like.

Exercise: walking outside for at least 30-60 minutes a day.

Yoga: it balances your energy at the body-mind-spirit level. Before my residency I completed the Inner Engineering Isha Yoga Program, designed by Sadhguru.[14] What I'd always wanted was to experience an advanced four-day yoga program called BSP (Bhava Spandana)[15] but never had the chance. It intrigued me, since Sadhguru designed it to help you go beyond the limitations of body and mind and experience higher levels of consciousness. People who attended it were very impressed, but kept a vow of silence about it.

I thought that this was my chance and went there during my journey. The age range of program participants was from 17 to 80 years old and it was a tremendous experience. Choose any type of yoga for yourself, whichever makes you feel comfortable.

Others: There are of course many other options. You might try an infrared sauna, which provides intensive detox and is used in some clinics in Europe and Mexico. Another option is hydrotherapy/hot and

---

[13] (https://www.herbdoc.com/index.php/?c=1)
[14] (http://www.ishayoga.org/introductory-programs/inner-engineering).
[15] http://www.ishayoga.org/advanced-programs/bhava-spandana

cold-water therapy used in Dr. Shulze's program. Also you can just stand on the ground and feel the earth through your bare feet, drink clean water, and generally do healthy things.

CHAPTER TWENTY-ONE:

You Are Love

"Neither a lofty degree of intelligence nor imagination nor both together go to the making of genius. Love, love, love, that is the soul of genius."
—*Wolfgang Amadeus Mozart*

It is an incredible journey, to finally find oneself on the other side of the fence, facing an "incurable" disease. If you fully immerse yourself in it, trust your fate, believe in yourself, listen to your heart and follow your soul, you can make many discoveries.

What I felt was that on one side of that fence people were living their normal lives—as we all did for many years, believing in the material world—but then, on the other side of the fence, a gathering storm was coming toward us all, one that would wash away the old consciousness of the world and awaken people. On a crest of this wave are spiritually advanced people such as Panache Desai, Greg Braden, Caroline Myss,

Dr. Wayne W. Dyer, Dr. Deepak Chopra, Bruce Lipton, Louise Hay and others with a higher awareness and realization of the world.

It seems that a time of change has been coming, bringing more and more evidence of the truth. And even then, even so, it's difficult for our logical minds to accept.

Yet there's so much impressive evidence that's hard to refute. Evidence is in the books of Dr. Eben Alexander[16] and Anita Moorjani.[17] Both of them had near-death experiences induced by deep coma. They "crossed the border" into another dimension and, through connection with universal consciousness/intelligence, obtained a deep understanding of who we are and what the world is. They came back with a new belief system, understanding and perception of the world, in order to deliver a message of truth to people.

I would like to join this wave and give my hands to those facing cancer, fighting desperately against it, crying from loneliness and fear of death. My message to you is the following: the truth is that you are not just a physical body; you are an infinite, perfect being. You have the power inside you to heal yourself! Cancer is a crisis of your soul. The soul is calling you, but you are trapped by your logical mind's fear and so you concentrate on your physical body treatment. Cancer of the physical body is an indicator of your inner state. Your magnificent soul can't live anymore the way you do and you need to free yourself from all painful emotions, and toxic/negative exposure—and upgrade or download a new advanced system of beliefs and attitudes toward the world.

Stop fighting, biting, blaming and hating and sharing "poor me" stories. Accept your cancer with love and celebrate it! Yes: celebrate that you are given the chance to be upgraded to a new you - become love! There is very deep meaning behind this attitude and you will be able to understand it when you move forward and dive within.

You are love, but you have lost your identity. Find it! The attitude of love is key for your healing. Love has a higher vibrational frequency and

---

[16] (an American neurosurgeon, author of *Proof of Heaven*)
[17] (http://anitamoorjani.com, author of *Dying to be Me*)

it's the frequency of your infinite being. It is the language of your soul! The energy at which you vibrate (feelings which you are experiencing) is the language you use to talk to the universe.

What you will ask for and give out (the level of frequency you vibrate) will be given back to you (you attract the same frequency wave) and will manifest itself as a solid form in the physical world. When you are able to release all painful feelings that are burning you inside, you will become a master of your every thought and feeling, of the way that you act in every moment. You will learn to think from the heart and maintain an attitude of love and your cancer melt away and never ever come back again. If you become love, your energy begins to vibrate at a frequency that is in direct alignment with the divine energy of the fifth dimension ... and true miracles start to happen.

In December 2012, the earth and humanity went through a transitional shift in general consciousness. We have entered the fifth dimension, which is the dimension of love - true, unconditional love.

What does this mean? A dimension isn't a place, but rather a state of consciousness with specific frequencies of vibrations that provide certain opportunities for us. The third dimension (level of consciousness) we lived in before was the dimension of the limited logical mind with rigid beliefs, attitudes and rules. We lived in duality (right/wrong, good/bad, like/don't like) and thought that this was the only way of thinking. In the third dimension we perceived time as a linear movement from past to future - and everything was conditional.

The concept of unconditional love couldn't exist there.

We perceived the third dimension through our left-side brain, which is the home of the logical mind. It knows what it knows—and doesn't know what it doesn't know.

The "end of the world" in December 2012 meant the end of the third dimension (level of old consciousness/how we were thinking, feeling and acting) and a shift to a higher dimension: a new level of consciousness with higher frequency vibrations.

The fifth dimension has a level of frequency of universal creation and is the dimension of unconditional love. If you reach this dimension (it is a level of consciousness, which means the way of thinking, feeling, acting), you will be able to receive everything easily and effortlessly.

It is a new state of being.

These higher frequencies are available now and anyone can experience them if they can resonate with them. The laws of physics of the third dimension can't be applied to the fifth dimension and our logical mind can't understand the journey we are now on.

What is important to understand is that we can move into this dimension only when we release all our emotional and mental baggage from the third dimension, leave the old way of thinking, feeling, and acting, and become masters of our minds - we will be able to control our every thought and feeling at every moment.

Your vibrational frequency (feelings you have inside) is what determines your ability to access the perception world of the fifth dimension. When you are able to do it, you will enter radiant health, unconditional love and abundance. Love is the key to everything!

Now we are all waking from the illusion of our physical world and are beginning to see that we are not just a physical body, but multidimensional beings: infinite beings in the physical body functioning through the mind and operating in two different dimensions, universe and planet earth, which *are very powerful.*

The truth is that there is no death of the infinite being and you will know it when you awaken.

FINAL NOTES FOR THOSE FACING CANCER

Dear friends,

I want to emphasize that even though an elaboration of the spiritual approach to illness is primary to my way of thinking, medical treatment *should* be considered, and my experience described in this book shouldn't be taken as advice for your specific situation.

You have to make your own choice, take responsibility for it, and decide which way you will go: you will either follow traditional medicine, non-traditional medicine, or a combination of both. It's very important to make this decision from the comfort zone of your belief system.

Looking back, I can see that when I was diagnosed with cancer, I could accept *only* standard protocol treatments, not alternative ones. In order for me to admit a new vision of reality and change my mind about it, I had to go through a deep transformative process leading me to the discovery of who I am (Infinite perfect being=Soul=Love=Light=Energy, who needs a physical body to exist on earth and a mind to function) and the realization of the main principles of the body, mind and spirit interconnection. This discovery allowed me to tune into the healing power from within, which every human being has, and set me on a pathway towards complete recovery.

Since my "experiment" wasn't clean, and I have been using both chemotherapy and alternative treatment, some may say that I can't prove whether my recovery was due to standard treatment protocol or other modalities.

Let's pause here for a minute and think: are we talking about complete resolution of the tumor on an MRI, or are we talking about complete recovery? I am fully aware of and acknowledge the fact that chemotherapy is always prescribed based on the cancer cell/tissue pathology result, and as a scientifically developed weapon it is highly effective in destroying and killing cancer cells. No doubt that in some cases using *only* chemotherapy can lead to complete resolution of the tumor on an MRI. But what is next? We just did "symptomatic" treatment by destroying the tumor with chemotherapy at the level of the physical body (which is a soul suitcase) but we didn't address the source of the disease—and as a result, we know that the cancer can come back at any time.

So what's next? Next is chemo, surgery and radiation to poison, cut, and burn it even more, to "prevent" it from coming back. And what's next? Three, five, ten years of survival, maybe more ...

What I am trying to say is that it doesn't matter how you reach complete resolution of the tumor on an MRI, either by following the standard protocol or using alternative treatment - it is your choice and your journey. Either way, you will be able to reach recovery once you learn how to address the other two levels of your Higher Being (mind and spirit), recognize the wholeness of this unity, and go through a process of deep inner transformation.

Pushing someone in a certain direction (either traditional or non-traditional) can create resistance and do more harm than good.

The main point of this book is to show those who are facing incurable diseases that cancer can't be cured *only* by chemo/surgery and radiation (when it is *only* directed toward the physical body) without the involvement of mind and spirit. We are energetic, multidimensional beings and the cure for cancer lies through understanding, recognition and acceptance of ourselves as whole human beings through body, mind, and spirit vision. This is the most important message to receive from this book.

The body-mind-spirit approach described in this book shows you how this unity works and provides directions to navigate it. It's very important to understand that diet, detox, releasing, meditation and prayers are *only* tools that you require in order to uncover your inner potential and bring changes within yourself. It requires a strong belief, desire and determination to make it happen.

Don't foolishly expect a full recovery by doing all these things if you are still holding on to painful memories and emotions, judging, blaming, and resisting change. Your path will lead you to success when, using these tools, you're able to return your energy through radical forgiveness, letting go, changing your perception and accepting the world and people the way they are. It's important to understand that body, mind and spirit philosophy doesn't mean you should expect healing just by following a diet, detox, or meditation. It means that, using these tools, you will unlock your inner power and go through a deep transformation process.

If you undergo chemo/surgery and radiation and want to achieve complete recovery, you should consider the body-mind-spirit approach and address changes necessary for your mind and spirit. Since the physical, mental and spiritual elements of your being are crucially interrelated, you can't win over cancer if those levels of your whole being are not attuned and balanced. You can't heal the body with a sick mind. Your noisy mind, which plays an instrumental role in your well-being and recovery, is overloaded with painful emotions (anxiety, fear of death, insecurity, anger, unhappy relationships, past memories) is constantly fighting with cancer and making you suffer even more. To make a miracle happen and become free from cancer, you need to accept your multidimensionality, your wholeness, and for that reason, you may use the tools described in this book. Those tools will guide you on how to clean your body, release emotional pain, forgive, quiet your mind, and connect to your higher self.

We are all witnesses that miracles happen and cancer patients have been healed.
This miracle is not about which choice you make regarding your treatment (traditional or non-traditional) it is about how you will approach it regardless of the choice. It is about your belief, determination and desire.

Here's a table that lays out this guidance for you:

Whole being Body-Mind-Spirit level	Cancer patient reality	What should be done for complete recovery	Tools (how it can be done)	Expected outcome (healing)
I. SPIRITUAL	**Lost connection with higher self** Most patients began to pray, some do meditation	**Need to connect with a higher self** Through prayers (surrender to God), Meditation, Energy transmission	**Prayer** (connect to higher self) **Meditation** (help to quiet your mind, release) **Energy transmission** (transmission of divine energy to induce healing)	**Connection with a higher self** Discovery of self love, love to others and life Changes in perception of the world
II. MENTAL	**NOISY MIND** **Painful emotions** anxiety, anger, stress, unhappy relationship, financial problems, fear of death, insecurity **Draining past memories** most often originating in childhood **Toxic attitudes** fighting cancer, judging, blaming yourself/others	**QUIET YOUR MIND** Need to be consciously aware of your thoughts, Drop negative thoughts Reprogram your mind for love and health **RELEASING:** Let go of painful emotions and forgive Learn to be grateful (the power of gratitude and forgiveness clean the blockages) Stop fighting cancer, but love it! (fighting cancer causes resistance and holds on it, loving cancer keeps it away from you). Healing unhealthy attitudes and toxic decisions. Stop blaming and judging Focus on a positive outcome. Believe in your recovery. Celebrate!	**TOOLS** EFT, Larry Crane's releasing techniques and others Become consciously aware of your thoughts and feelings Yoga Breathing techniques Positive affirmation Mantras Chanting Visualization Singing Laughing	**BECOME A MASTER OF YOUR MIND** Discover the nature of your wound and come to the realization of why you have been hurt Clean blockages. Restore your energy through radical forgiveness, letting go and acceptance of the world and people the way they are.
III. PHYSICAL	TRADITIONAL TREATMENT **Chemo-surgery-radiation** feeling pain, low energy and other symptoms NON TRADITIONAL **Diet, detox, etc.**	Talk to your doctor regarding diet and find out if you can combine detox with your treatment or not Choose a program which you like and stick to it (diet and detox must be on the list)	Diet Detox walking/exercise, swimming, hydrotherapy infrared sauna, etc.	Healthy body

Body-Mind-Spirit unity

Soul

Perfect Infinite Being
Love
Higher Self
Light

Mind

The instrument of the Soul enabling it to function in a physical body and create our world

Body

The Souls's shell created to experience reality on Earth

Cancer

Soul "crysis"

1. lost self identity
2. absence of self love
3. old system of beliefs and attitudes towards the world is shutting down....

"Sick" Mind

1. painful emotions
2. negtive thoughts, past traumatic memories

"Sick" Body

"Sick" thoughts patterns coupled with feelings accumulate and block the flow of vital energy through the body

Body-Mind-Spirit approach

Soul

1. surrender to God
2. find self identity
3. discover self love
4. "download" new, advanced system of beliefs and attitudes towards the world

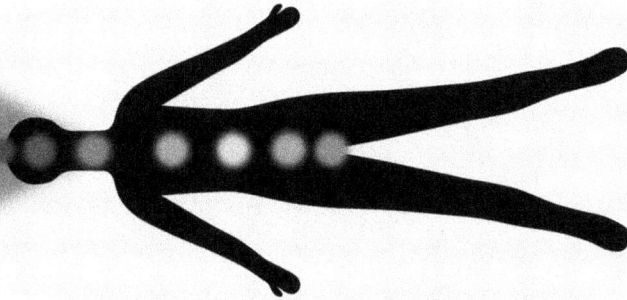

Mind

1. radical forgiveness, letting go and acceptance
2. become a master of your mind
3. love your cancer (fighting cancer creates resistance)

Body

Standard protocol treatment — Alternative treatment

YOUR CHOICE

A MESSAGE FROM THE BLACK SWAN

Cancer is curable!

*

For ages, our limited perception of the world didn't let us see the truth of who we really are, and cancer remained "incurable" because the physical body was the target of treatments.

*

We are not just our physical bodies: we are infinite, perfect, multidimensional beings.

*

Cancer can be cured when it's recognized, understood and accepted through all levels of the multidimensional approach of the body-mind-spirit unity.

*

You have the power inside to heal yourself. You must learn how to dive within, to rediscover your true core self, your courage and your trust.

*

The total resolution of cancer on the physical level, as evidenced on a MRI, doesn't mean a complete cure. A deep fear of recurrence of the disease continues to live inside us. Radical forgiveness, acceptance, and letting go are the tools that will lead you to change your perception of the world. This in turn will free you from your fear … and that's when you will have the freedom of full recovery.

*

Love is the essence of our soul: it's our inherent state of self, of ourselves as infinite beings. We're unconsciously trying, all our lives, to return to this joyful inherent state, but the sad part is that we're usually blindly looking in the wrong direction.

*

Love is the key to all healing. Be love, and live your life through love.

EPILOGUE

I can't believe that almost two years have already passed since my world turned upside down because of this disease and I was blown away from my residency by the wind of change. I'll always remember the day when I got this news, sank to my knees and prayed . . .

In my prayers I accepted my trial, thanked God for my path, and promised to learn what I needed to and go through it whatever turn it might take. I didn't fear death at all and somewhere deep in my Soul I knew that I was healthy and that I needed to embark on a journey to find the answer of what love is.

I never thought that while going through this challenge, searching for love and looking for the "root" cause of cancer, I would find answers to questions that I'd never dreamed of, and that I'd go through such a deep transformation that my whole life would be changed.

My physical appearance, taste, style, and image have changed, along with my attitudes, beliefs, job, relationship, and physical location. Now a new healthy and happy woman with curly dark brown hair looks at me from the mirror and initially I didn't know much about her. I hesitated for a while, then welcomed and accepted a new me with gratitude, and let a new Marina be.

When you see the light at the end of tunnel, when you were told (and believed) that all you could expect was the stone over your grave, you feel peace, freedom and gratitude to God for your journey. Who knows if my soul preset my journey for me or not? But Lynda Hill was right: my soul has a message to pass on to people and I am stretching out my hands with this book to those in need.

With love,
Marina

ACKNOWLEDGMENTS

I would like to express my gratitude to my dear parents, family, residency and those who in some way or another have been part of this journey.

To my dear parents: Thank you for being there for me on this journey and caring for me. I am grateful to my dearest mother, who surrounded me with unconditional love and became a partner on my journey. I am grateful to my father who suffered silently, but always believed in me.

To my husband and son, whose lives were shaken and turned upside down along with mine. Thank you for being next to me at the most difficult time and letting me follow my heart. To my husband's aunt, who truly cared for me.

To my sister Irina and my friend Annie, my guiding stars at my times of desperation during my disease: I would never have been able to overcome this experience by myself. Thank you.

To my residency program, program director, residents, colleagues from the hospital and those medical staff who took care of me. I was deeply touched by the continuing support, care and love given to me. I would like to express my gratitude to all of you for your compassion and support.

ABOUT THE AUTHOR

Marina was born in Kazakhstan, where she completed her medical school, followed by a neurology residency. While in Kazakhstan she not only worked as an attending neurologist, but later became the first coordinator-physician of the US Public Health program through the United States Peace Corps.

In 2003 Marina immigrated to Canada with her family and was subsequently accepted into an Internal Medicine Residency in the United States.

She started her North American path of licensure, helped countless patients during her medical residency program up until 2011. Midway through her third year of residency she was diagnosed with stage 3 breast cancer and had to face the biggest challenge of her life. She began a journey which led her to the discovery of the healing Truth and creation of her first book *Message from the Black Swan.*

Website: marinawassermann.com

www.ingramcontent.com/pod-product-compliance
Lightning Source LLC
Chambersburg PA
CBHW052109090426
42741CB00009B/1734